Septuagint:

Job

Septuagint, Volume 16

SCRIPTURAL RESEARCH INSTITUTE
Published by Digital Ink Productions, 2024

Copyright

Septuagint: Job

Third edition. November 25, 2024

Copyright © 2024 Scriptural Research Institute.

ISBN: 978-1-998636-08-2

The Septuagint was translated into Greek at the Library of Alexandria between 250 and 132 BC.

This English translation was created by the Scriptural Research Institute in 2019 through 2024, through the comparison of most published copies of Septuagint manuscripts. Additionally, the Leningrad Codex, Aleppo Codex, Peshitta, Coptic and Ge'ez Bibles, Targum on Job, Dead Sea Scrolls, and Papyrus Oxyrhynchus 3522, were used for comparative analysis.

The image used for the cover is an artistic reinterpretation of "Job" by Léon Bonnat, painted in 1880. The original painting is currently located as the Musée d'Orsay, in Paris (RF 487).

Table of Contents

TABLE OF CONTENTS

TABLE OF CONTENTS

Forward

In the mid 3rd century BC, King Ptolemy II Philadelphus of Egypt ordered a translation of the ancient Israelite scriptures for the Library of Alexandria, which resulted in the creation of the Septuagint. It is generally accepted that there were several versions of the ancient Israelite scriptures before the translation of the Septuagint. The Book of Job is a curiosity among the Israelite texts as it is not about one of the ancient Israelite patriarchs. However, in later commentaries on the book, Job was said to have lived around the time of Abraham. The Dead Sea Scroll 4QpaleoJob^c proves that the Book of Job was in use among Judeans before the transition to the Aramaic "block letter" script circa 140 BC. However, the Hebrew translation found in the Masoretic text has many Aramaic loanwords, indicating it was translated from an Aramaic book of Job.

The version of Job found in the Septuagint, Masoretic text, and Peshitta, all appear to be copies of a standardized version of the Book of Job that was circulating in Judea under Greek rule, and during the Hasmonean and Herodian dynasties. Fragments of it have been found among the Dead Sea Scrolls, written in Canaanite, Hebrew, and Aramaic, dated to between 330 BC and 44 AD. The Canaanite texts appear to be the oldest, generally dated to between 330 and 165 BC, while the Hebrew and Aramaic fragments date to later times, generally dated to between 165 BC and 44 AD. The Canaanite text found in the Dead Sea Scrolls is generally attributed to the Samaritans, however, some take a broader view that Judahites may have also been using the Canaanite script at the time, parallel with Aramaic.

As the surviving Samaritan religion doesn't include Job as a religious figure, the question of who used these Canaanite texts continues to be disputed. According to Josephus, the Essen sect believed their ancestors had lived in Judea for a thousand generations, which meant that they did not enter Canaan with the Israelites, and therefore they could be interpreted as Canaanites and may have also been using this script. Another theory regarding the usage of the Canaanite script in Judea under Greek rule is that it was used by a nationalist faction that was trying to rekindle the cultural relationship with Carthage, the last land where the Canaanite script was in use.

Whoever was using the Phoenician script, the surviving fragments found among the Dead Sea Scrolls are remarkably consistent with the Septuagint, Peshitta, and Masoretic versions of the Book of Job, which proves that the text was standardized before the Septuagint was translated at the Library of Alexandria. Nevertheless, while the books are remarkably similar across languages, there are noticeable forms of the book, with chapter structure details changing in different versions of the book. Three of these versions of Job are found within the Septuagint manuscripts, and each overlapped with variations of the book that were translated into Hebrew, Syriac, Coptic, and Latin.

Separate Greek translations were likely made from both Aramaic and a language that used the Canaanite script, however, it is not clear which Canaanite dialect the book was written in. The Greek manuscripts include words that are transliterations of Aramaic words, Hebrew words, and some other forms of Canaanite. The Hebrew words are easily explained by the Christian attempts to correct the names in the Septuagint through comparison to the Hebrew translation in the late Classical era, however, there is no obvious source for the other Canaanite words.

While the Greek and Hebrew translations of Job are extremely similar, there are some significant differences, such as the Hebrew use of the name Yhůh (יהוה), versus the Greek use of the term Lord (Κυρίου). This is consistent with other books in the Septuagint, as well as sections of the Masoretic text that remain in Aramaic, where the term lord (אדני) is used instead of Yhůh (יהוה). Fragments of a copy of the Septuagint's Job were discovered in the 1800s known as Papyrus Oxyrhynchus 3522, which date to the 1st century AD and include the name Yhŭh (𐤉𐤄𐤅𐤄), however, the name is in the Phoenician script spliced into the Greek text, indicating it was a later redaction of the Septuagint. Additionally, the Septuagint's copy of Job includes some text copied from the Aramaic Book of Job at the end of the translation of the Canaanite book.

Nevertheless, the surviving Hebrew translation of Job includes many Aramaic loanwords, which indicates the Canaanite version of Job was translated from an Aramaic text. One of the more obvious pieces of evidence of the Aramaic source text is the name of Elihu (אליהוא), whose name is Aramaic for "God is Yhŭ," the Aramaic form of Yhŭh. Elihu is considered by some scholars to be the author of the Book of Job, however, others believe that his speech in chapters 32 through 37 was added later. He is notable in that he was not mentioned at all previously in this book, and disappears after the Lord starts speaking to the other three kings in chapter 38.

In the Book of Job, Elihu takes the contrary view to the three kings who are berating Job, and ultimately the Lord punishes them. This is the exact opposite outcome from the Testament of Job, where Elihu is the one berating Job, and punished by the Lord. The Testament of Job contains the Song of Eliphaz, which appears to have been composed before 1800 BC, and claims to have been written by Nahor, the brother of Abraham, and father of Elihu, which seems to be an attempt by the author of the Testament of Job to give it priority over the Book of Job. If Elihu produced the redacted version of Job, adding himself and his opinion to the story, then it was likely when the book was translated into Aramaic.

The Aramaic translation of Job was likely produced sometime between 747 and 656 BC, during the Nubian 25th Dynasty of Egypt, as Egypt is not mentioned, however, Kush is. At the time, the Empire of Kush, based in modern Sudan, ruled Egypt, and so the land of Egypt would have been included in any reference to Kush. During this era, the Neo-Assyrian Empire conquered the Kingdom of Samaria in 720 BC and relocated the Israelite population. The Assyrians then attacked the Kingdom of Judah and laid siege to Jerusalem in 701 BC, but the Kushites attacked the Assyrians in support of Judah, and the Assyrians withdrew.

This Assyrian invasion of Judah was during the reign of King Hezekiah, who initiated the first major overhaul of the religion of Judah, destroying Moses' bronze serpent statue and the Asherah trees, in King Solomon's Temple, in favor of promoting the god Yhủh. Hezekiah was one of the better-documented kings of Judah, partly because Judah was pulled into the imperial intrigue of the Neo-Assyrian and Kushite Empires, and partly because he was a prolific builder. The Siloam Tunnel and part of the Broad Wall he built in Jerusalem still exist. Sennacherib's Prism, a document discovered in the ruins of Nineveh, and dating back to the siege of Jerusalem confirms the siege from the Assyrian perspective, and names Hezekiah as the king of Judah.

Evidence for the religious reforms of Hezekiah has also been found in the archaeological ruins of ancient Judah, such as the central cult room of the temple at Arad, an ancient Judahite fortress, where the altars were carefully disassembled and buried under a plaster floor as if the priests expected to reassemble them again in the future. The Yahwist reforms of Hezekiah's reign were reversed under the rule of his son King Manasseh (697 to 687 BC), who also forged close relations with the Neo-Assyrian Empire, and according to 4th Kingdoms (Masoretic Kings) records, the old gods of the Israelites began being worshiped again.

This continued under Manasseh's son Amon (אָמוֹן), who was named after the dominant Kushite god Amanai (𓏏𓈖𓈖𓂝𓇋), known in Egypt as Amen (𓇋𓏠𓈖). However, Amon's son Josiah returned to the Yahwism of his great-grandfather and destroyed the restored statue of Ba'al and Asherah trees from the Temple again. This ultimately led to an Egyptian invasion of Judah, which the author of 1st Ezra claimed was so Pharaoh Necho II could restore the worship of God in the Temple. As Necho II is well documented in the ruins of Egypt as a worshiper of the Nubian sun god Amanai, the South Egyptian sun god Amen, and the North Egyptian sun god Atum (☒), it supports the claim that he restored the worship of the original god of the Temple of Solomon, the Canaanite sun god Shalim. Both the city of Jerusalem, known as Úru Šalim^ki (☒), meaning 'light of Shalim' in Amorite Cuneiform, and King Solomon were named after the sun god Shalim, who, like Atum, Amen, and Amanai, was associated with the setting sun.

Like Atum, Amen, and Amanai, the Ba'al worshiped at Solomon's Temple was married to a wife referred to as the 'hand of god,' who was worshiped by planting sacred trees. In Egypt and Nubia, the sun god and his wife were also viewed as the parents of the moon god, the Nubian Khasa (☒), South Egyptian Khonsu (☒), and North Egyptian Iohu (☒), suggesting that the son of Ba'al and Asherah in Jerusalem was a moon god named Yhŭ, however, this has yet to be proven conclusively. The only archaeologically attested title for the son of Ba'al and Asherah in Jerusalem was Adonay, however, the pottery shards found at Kuntillet Ajrud do confirm that Yhŭh was considered the son of Asherah circa 800 BC.

The pottery shards include references to Yhŭh being worshiped in Samaria and Edom and depict Yhŭh as a calf god, and Asherah as a heifer. This suggests that the statues of heifers worshiped in Samaria at the time, were depictions of Asherah. The kingdom of Edom, and the Levite city of Libnah, in the borderlands of Judah, Edom, and Egypt, had both declared independence from Judah in the 840s BC over a religious dispute and claimed that the wrong god was being worshiped in Solomon's Temple. Libnah was the city where the later Yahwist priesthood emerged from in the 700s BC, supporting the name of Adony being Yahweh.

Meanwhile, in Edom, the name of their god transitioned from Yhŭh to Qŭś (𐤒𐤅𐤔) over the following two centuries. Since Yhŭh and Qŭś are described identically in the literature from the era, most historians accept that the Edomites changed the name of Yhŭh to Qŭś in the centuries after becoming independent. As the Nubians were dominating Egypt during this era, and had close trade relations with the Edomites, the source of the name Qŭś, was likely the Nubian name Khasa, confirming that Yhŭh was considered the Israelite moon before the breakup of the united kingdom of Judah and Edom.

If Elihu was the Aramaic translator, he had to have lived sometime during the era of the Nubian 25th

Dynasty of Egypt, which was a time of great cultural turmoil in Canaan. The Assyrians were conquering everything they could, and Samaria fell to them in 721 BC, resulting in most Israelites being forced to relocate to other parts of the Neo-Assyrian Empire. While some of the ancient Canaanite and Israelite texts had already been translated into Aramaic before the Assyrians conquered Aram, most of the ancient texts that had been written in Canaanite were translated after Samaria fell, and it is likely that the Book of Job would have been translated into Aramaic at this time. However, there were at least two versions of the Book of Job in Aramaic, as the Greek translators added a synopsis of Job's genealogy at the end of their translation of the Canaanite version, which they report was found in the Aramaic Book of Job. The Aramaic Book of Job they were referring to no longer exists, however, another book about Job has survived to the present, the Testament of Job, which also seems to have drawn from the Aramaic Book of Job.

The version of Job's life found in the Testament of Job is generally consistent with the other surviving books of Job, however, includes details about Job's life not found in the book of Job. Some of these details are consistent with the Aramaic Book of Job mentioned in the subscription at the end of the Septuagint's Book of Job, however, not all details are consistent. The subscription

at the end of Job was either added by the original translators, or someone else later on, but is accepted as having
been added in the BC era. A similar subscription is found
in ancient Arabic copies of Job, however, these were
likely translated from Greek. The details included in the
subscription are not found in the version of Job found in
the Syriac Peshitta Bible, and therefore it is assumed the
text is now lost.

The Aramaic version does not appear to have been the
original version of Job, as it contains loanwords that
appear to be transliterations of Akkadian cuneiform
terms, meaning it was translated from a cuneiform text
at some point. One of the most obvious examples of this is
the name of the land Job lived in. In the Hebrew translation found in the Masoretic Text, it is called "the land of
Ôûṣ" (בְּאֶרֶץ־עֶוּץ), while in the Septuagint, it is transliterated as the "land of Aysitidi" (χώρα τη Αυσίτιδι). As
neither Ouz nor Aysitidi appears to have been a known
land in the Classical Era, the Greek and Hebrew translators must have transliterated what was in the Canaanite
texts they were working from. The beginning of the
Greek translation of the name, Ays (Αυσ), is a transliteration of the same term found in the Hebrew translation
Ôûṣ (עֶוּץ), while the rest of the word, itidi (ίτιδι), appears
to be a transliteration of the cuneiform term itiatu
(𒂊𒋫𒀸𒈾𒈨), meaning boundaries, environs, or region.

The Hebrew translators appear to have recognized that the Canaanite text read "the land of Ôûṣ-land," and dropped the second reference to Ôûṣ being a land, while the Greek translators simply transliterated the name as they saw it.

This transliteration error, resulting in "land of Ôûṣ-land," could not have originated in the Canaanite version of Job, as the same term is found in the Testament of Job, which appears to have been translated into Greek from Aramaic, meaning the error must have entered into the text when it was translated into Aramaic from cuneiform. Cuneiform was the script used in ancient Canaan during the Egyptian New Kingdom Era, as evidenced by the Amarna Letters. Therefore, any Israelite books written in the era would have almost certainly been written in cuneiform. In northern Canaan, in the region around Mount Zephon, a variant of cuneiform was known as Ugaritic, which was a precursor to the Phoenician and Aramaic scripts. The surviving Ugaritic Texts report that many of the holy books used in the town of Ugarit were translations of Egyptian copies of ancient Canaanite texts.

It's unclear why Egyptian translations of Canaanite texts were being re-translated into Canaanite during the New Kingdom era, however, the older Canaanite script, called the Byblos syllabary, had been lost by that era, and so it is possible that many Canaanite texts had been lost. Additionally, the imposition of the cuneiform script by the Hyksos 15ᵗʰ dynasty and later the Mitanni Empire may have also resulted in the loss of traditional Canaanite texts. Canaan had been part of the Egyptian Middle Kingdom, when many of the Egyptian translations had probably been made, as well as the later Canaanite 14ᵗʰ dynasty of Egypt, and so many ancient Canaanite texts had probably been translated into Egyptian before being restored to Canaan during the New Kingdom.

The lost Cuneiform Book of Job appears to have been one of the books restored during the New Kingdom, as the Masoretic version of Job contains obscure Egyptian terms, indicating it was once written in Egyptian hiero-glyphs or hieratic. Hieratic was the handwritten form of hieroglyphs, and both systems were in use throughout the Old, Middle, and New Kingdom eras of Egyptian history, before finally being replaced by Demotic during the Late Period. Generally, hieroglyphs were used for official government and temple decrees, while hieratic was used for most other purposes, which strongly suggests the Egyptian version of Job was in hieratic, not hieroglyphs.

There are several Ancient Egyptian terms in the Book of Job that indicate it was once in hieratic, however, it does not appear to have been written in the

Egyptian language, but rather, another language, presumably Canaanite, using the hieratic script. While there are several Egyptian terms in Job, none is more well documented than the word Behemoth, spelled as bhmût (ܒܗܡܘܬܐ / בהמות) in both the Masoretic and Peshitta's version of Job. In the Septuagint, the word was translated as "beasts" (θηρία), which is the same translation used in the Targum from the era, the Aramaic language text intended to explain the Hebrew translations of the Tanakh to the Aramaic-speaking population of Judea.

The term bhmût is itself accepted as being an Aramaic plural form of bhmû (עמהלך), however, that word is not found in any known Aramaic text. For almost 2000 years, linguists have considered this a transliteration of the Ancient Egyptian word pảỉhmû (𓄿𓏏𓎛𓐝𓈖═), meaning "water ox." This translation was worked out during the Early Christian Era, and assumed to be a reference to a hippopotamus, based on the conceptually similar words meaning hippopotamus in Greek, Arabic, Persian, Hebrew, and Coptic, all of which are composed of words meaning "horse" and either "water" or "river."

In this case, the verse seems to be referring both to actual hippopotamuses that lay in marshes, and also the Egyptian asterism of Taweret, named after a goddess who combined the forms of a hippopotamus and a crocodile. Taweret was one of the asterisms in the far north. Taweret was a very ancient goddess whose worship was widespread throughout Egypt, Nubia, Canaan, and the Minoan civilization. This common Egyptian form was depicted as an upright walking hippopotamus with a long crocodile tale. She was described in the Egyptian Book of Day and Night from the late Bronze Age as the guardian of the leg of Sutekh, their name for the Big Dipper. The Hyksos dynasty, which had ruled both Egypt and Canaan during the middle Bronze Age, had equated the Egyptian god Sutekh, with the Canaanite god Seth, and the Amorite god Hadad, collectively known as Ba'al, meaning "Lord." As a northern asterism, Taweret was at the opposite end of the sky from the Leviathan (Yam, Cetus), which was on the southern horizon, explaining the opposing yet coupled relationships of the beings in the texts that mention them.

Whatever the word Behemoth represented to the authors, it continued to be used in Hebrew and Aramaic literature until at least 200 BC. In the Book of Enoch, Behemoth was reported to live in a desert east of Eden, which may have been a metaphor, or a reference to an eastern desert. This may have been an ancient reference to dinosaur bones being dug up in the Gobi Desert. Ancient texts such as the Shennong Bencaojing prescribe the use of 'dragon bones' in Chinese medicine, which were no doubt excavated from the Gobi Desert, as they are today. Although it is unclear when King Shennong lived, his life is traditionally dated to 2437 BC. The medical text attributed to him, the Shennong Bencaojing, has existe

The link between the Ancient Egyptian word for "water buffalo" and the Aramaic term "bhmǔ" was worked out in the late Classical Era, and therefore influenced the languages within the Byzantine and Russian Empires, resulting in the words for "hippopotamus" being derived from behemoth in many languages, including Armenian begemot (բեգեմոտ), Azerbaijani begemot, Belarusian bjehjemót (бегемóт), Bulgarian begemót (бегемóт), Chuvash begemot (бегемот), Georgian behemoti (ბეჰემოთი), Hebrew behemót (בְּהֵמוֹת), Kazakh begemot (бегемот), Kyrgyz begemot (бегемот), Latvian behemots, Lithuanian begemotas, Ossetian begemot (бегемот), Russian begemót (бегемóт), Tajik bahmut (баҳмут), Turkmen begemot, Ukrainian behemót (бегемóт), Uyghur bëgëmot (بېگېموت), and Uzbek begemot. In some of these languages, the term is now considered dated and has been replaced with words based on the Greek word hippopotamos (ἱπποπόταμος).

The Ancient Egyptians had several names for "hippopotamus," however, generally called it a ḥåb (𓎛𓄿𓃀), and therefore, while the Book of Job may have been written in Egyptian hieratic at one point, it probably wasn't written in the Egyptian language, suggesting it was written in Canaan during the Middle Kingdom, or in northern Egypt during the Canaanite (13ᵗʰ) dynasty. In any event, sometime before the New Kingdom Era, when the term ss yåůr (ꝗꝗꝗꝗ ꝛꝛ), meaning "horse of the Nile," was adopted by the Canaanites as a name for the hippopotamus. The Canaanite term is virtually identical to the two Egyptian words ssm (𓂝𓃀𓏏), meaning "horse," and ı̇trů (𓇋𓐁𓄿𓈖), meaning "great river," suggesting the term was also used in Late Egyptian, however, it is undocumented before the Classical Era, when it is documented as htho ior (ⲑⲟⲟ ⲓⲟⲣ), meaning "horse" and "Nile" in Coptic Egyptian. The Canaanite term was imported to Median and Persian as "aspa ap" from the Avestan words aspa (سپایؤ) and ap (سپ), meaning "horse" and "water," and continues today in the Persian term for hippopotamus, asb-e âbi (اسب آبی). The Persian term appears to have been the basis of the Greek and Arabic terms hippopotamos (ἱπποπόταμος) and faras nahr (فرس نهر), both of which combine the words for "horse" and "river."

Another Egyptian term found in the Book of Job, along with the books of Genesis and Joshua, is the use of the Egyptian monetary unit generally referred to as a 'lamb.' It was a gold 'coin' shaped like a lamb which was in use since the Middle Kingdom along with the more common copper and silver ring-shaped "coins." In the Septuagint, this was translated literally, as "ewe lamb" (ἀμνάδα), which is a translation of the word qšyth (קשיטה) found in the Masoretic text, however, the word was rarely used in Hebrew or Phoenician Canaanite, and does not appear to have been generally used in Aramaic. The texts it survives in, are set in the late Bronze Age, including the books of Genesis and Joshua, in both of which it was used as a monetary unit. The word is accepted as an Egyptian loanword, specifically referring to an Ancient Egyptian monetary unit that was represented as a lamb in hieroglyphs circa 1100 BC. While this does not prove the Book of Job itself was written in hieratic, it does mean that the Egyptian monetary unit was in use when the book was either written or translated into hieratic.

At some point before the Book of Job was standardized, probably when it was translated into Aramaic, parts were either lost or intentionally redacted, including the end of the slanderer's story-line, the Leviathan's story, and the Behemoth's story, as well as the answer to the question: why does suffering exist? The question is raised but never answered. It was probably answered in the slanderer's ending, and possibly tied into the stories of the Leviathan and Behemoth, who the Lord was preparing to destroy before Job suddenly 'won the lottery' and the story ended. The statements that the slanderer had originally risen about Job turned out to be correct, as he did not continue to praise the Lord but complained bitterly about everything he'd lost.

The closest he came to worshiping the Lord, was when he referred to himself as dirt before the swirling storm god floating in front of him, although that appears to be more an act of fear than worship. Much must have been removed from the story for some reason, as in addition to the Lord losing his bet and thinking he won, the Leviathan's story was never ended, and the Behemoth was introduced but the story was not told. Additionally, the Lord never answered Job's questions, which should have followed the strange description of the steam-powered bronze-covered Leviathan, which itself seems more like a description of a submarine from a Jules Verne novel than a living being.

The structure of the Book of Job indicates that it had at least two authors, as the mid-section is poetry, while the opening and closing sections are written in prose. Specifically, the discussion between the Lord and the slanderer at the beginning, and everything after Elihu is introduced is in prose, indicating it was likely added later on, and some scholars have suggested it was Elihu who added it. This, however, does not explain the redactions, as they all fall within Elihu's prose sections, therefore, if Elihu added his introduction and conclusion to the original poetry, someone else came along later and cut out significant sections. This anti-Elihuist redactor could also be the source of the anti-Elihu sentiments in the Song of Eliphaz that was quoted in the Testament of Job.

In the Song of Eliphaz, there is a reference to the "Northern One" being a dragon, which is an astronomical reference to Thuban being the pole star. Thuban is in what is today called the Constellation of Draco, however, those stars were considered a dragon long before the creation of the zodiac by the Neo-Babylonians. The Greeks called the stars Ladon, a snake-like dragon which is accepted as being the Greek version of Lotan, a Canaanite multi-headed serpent-dragon from the second millennium BC. Between 3900 and 1800 BC, the star Thuban was the pole star, however, due to the ongoing precession of the equinoxes, it moved away from the celestial north pole. The term 'precession of the equinoxes' refers to the slight movement of the Earth each year that causes the stars to shift their position above us over approximately 26,000 years.

The Canaanite dragon Lotan is known from the Ugaritic Texts of Bronze Age Canaan that were discovered by archaeologists in the 1900s. He was a servant of Yam, the god of the sea in the Canaanite religion. These texts were lost for thousands of years, but some must have still been around circa 550 BC, as Isaiah appears to have quoted them, however, replaced the name Lotan with Leviathan. Clearly, Isaiah viewed the Leviathan as the same seven-headed serpent-dragon the Canaanites called Lotan, and therefore the serpent-dragon the Greeks called Ladon. In the Greek myths, Ladon was the serpent-dragon that guarded the apple tree in the Garden of the Hesperides, which, given the connection to ancient Canaan via Lotan, implies the Garden of the Hesperides and the Garden of Eden story share a Canaanite origin, although the Eden story also drew from Sumerian creation mythology.

The earliest recorded reference to someone called Job was an Egyptian record of a Canaanite chieftain named Job from around 2000 BC, however, there is no reason to assume this is the same Job. If it is the same Job, then any attempt to link him to the historic kingdoms of the 1st millennium, such as Edom, or Ma'in are pure affectations added whenever the texts were standardized in ancient Samaria or Judah, or later when the Septuagint was translated. For example, King Zophar was recorded in the Masoretic Text as coming from the city of Naamah, in Canaan, while in the Septuagint he was King of Ma'in, an ancient kingdom in modern Yemen. If the text is from the second or third millennium BC, a Canaanite city makes sense, but the kingdom in Yemen that would not exist for another millennium or longer does not.

The situation is the opposite with the stars though, as it appears someone redacted or replaced the names of the stars the version of Job found in the Masoretic Text after it was translated into Greek. This redaction and updating of star's names goes far beyond the Book of Job and also affects other books that likely originated in the Canaanite script, including the Book of Judges. The Greek translation of Job includes many references to the morning star or the evening star which are almost all missing from the Masoretic text.

The Septuagint has a strange reference to the Pleiades star cluster where the term morning star should be, as it is placed in opposition to the evening star, and in relation to a north star and the "chambers of the south," likely a reference to the Decans used in Egyptian astronomy since the 10th dynasty. The name Pleiades also shows up in the Masoretic Text, which is one of the few times these texts agree on the star's name, indicating this was the original name in the Canaanite version of Job, and it simply was not redacted in the Masoretic text.

The Pleiades were used for navigation throughout antiquity, as they rose in the east shortly after nightfall, and slowly moved across the sky all night. The Greek name Pleiades is derived from their word meaning "sail" (πλέω) because the Helical Rising of Pleiades indicated that it was safe to begin trading on the Mediterranean. This 'sailing season' was taught to the Greeks by the much older Canaanite civilization, who had been trading in the Mediterranean for over a thousand years before the Greek civilization emerged as the dominant culture in the region.

As the Greek translation treats the Pleiades star cluster as the morning star, this would date the text to the Middle Bronze Age, approximately 2300 BC, when the Babylonian star catalogs record the Pleiades, which they called the "stars of stars" (✸✸ ✸✸), were the morning stars at the vernal equinox. By the time the Greeks translated Job, it had been around 2000 years since the Pleiades were the morning stars, and therefore, they had no reason to refer to the Pleiades as the morning stars unless that was in the text they translated. The reference is in Job chapter 9, as part of a series of stars that seem to be indicating the "morning star," "evening star," "pole star," and "decans of the south." Unfortunately, no copies of Job have survived among the Dead Sea Scrolls which include chapters 1 through 11, so it is unclear when these redactions took place.

The Greek translation refers to Hesperus, the Greek name for the planet Venus at sunset, however, the

Canaanites are not recorded using a term like this, instead referring to Shalim, the god of dusk, suggesting there was a star or constellation in the text, which the Greeks interpreted as a star at dusk, and translated as Hesperus. The Hebrew version of the verse refers to Orion, in the form of Kesil, a derogatory term for Orion which translates as "fool." This is not the original Canaanite name for Orion, but a late Persian Era Hebrew name for the constellation, based on the idea that whoever worshiped it as God was a fool. The older Aramaic name of the asterism and constellation was Npylå (𐤍𐤋𐤀𐤉𐤋), where the Nephilim (Orionids) fell from each October. The Orionids are a meteor shower that happens each year, between October 2 and November 7, as the Earth passes through the debris left by Halley's Comet. Peaks of 70 meteors a minute have been recorded, and these meteors fall from the region of the sky where Orion's upstretched arm is located.

This was the same asterism that the Old Kingdom Era Egyptians called Sah, whom they believed was the "father of the gods (stars)," because he created new stars (gods) each October. It is worth noting that when the Pleiades were the morning stars at the vernal equinox, Orion was the evening stars that same day of the year, supporting the name Npylå as having originally been in the text the Greeks and Hebrews translated. As the name was no longer used by the time the Greeks translated the Book of Job, they would have substituted the term 'evening star,' which happened to be Hesperus, while the Hebrew translators clearly knew which constellation was being referred to, and translated it as 'fool.'

The other major change to the stars found in the Masoretic Text was the substitution of the Wagon for a star name that has not survived to the present. The Wagon was the Babylonian era name for the constellation known as Ursa Minor, the Little Bear. The Greeks originally knew this constellation as the Phoenician Bear, as they had learned to navigate by it from the Canaanites. The Phoenicians used the stars of Ursa Minor to point the way north because in the first millennium BC, there was no pole star, and they were the closest stars to true north. Before 1800 BC, Thuban was the pole star, however, after approximately 1793 BC, the sky had no clear pole star, and a variety of northern stars were used to point the general direction of the north. By the Babylonian era, circa 800 BC, the northern stars were in the region now known as Ursa Minor, which the Babylonians named the Wagon of Heaven (or Sky Wagon).

In this case, the name Wagon was used in the translations to replace a star with an unknown name, because it was a northern asterism, in a verse where it was placed in the opposite direction as the 'decans of the south.' The word the Greeks used to translate the original name was Arcturus, the name of the brightest star in the north, but not a star that has ever been a pole star. This implies the name of the original star in the text was no longer recognized by the Greeks, but it had once been a singular pole star, not a group of pole stars. As the Greeks had studied Babylonian astrology, and also had a word for 'wagon' they could not have found that word in the text they translated.

If they were translating a text that mentioned a singular pole star, it would place the origin of the texts before 1800 BC, when Thuban was the pole star. After 1800 BC there were no clear pole stars, and Kappa Draconis in Draco, Mizar in Ursa Major, Pherkad in Ursa Minor, and Kochab in Ursa Minor all wandered around the general vicinity of the pole, but none seems to have gotten closer than about 7° of true north until Polaris started approaching the north celestial pole in the 400s AD. In comparison, Polaris is currently about 0.5° of true north, and Thuban reached a peak of about 0.17° of true north in approximately 2830 BC. Thuban would have served as a pole star from approximately 3900 to 1800 BC.

The Song of Eliphaz, in the Testament of Job, also refers to the Northern One as a Dragon, which would seem to confirm that the pole star in question was Thuban, as Thuban is in the constellation of Draco, which the ancient Greeks had called Ladon, a name they had learned from the Canaanites, who called it Lotan. This implies that the origin of the story of Job dates back to the early 2nd millennium BC at the latest, and lends support to the idea that he is the Canaanite chieftain named Job the Egyptian records mentioned around 2000 BC.

The fundamental problem with dating the story of Job to 2000 BC, or any time before the Israelites invaded Canaan, is that the story of Job is no longer an Israelite or Jewish story, which many Jews and Christians would categorically reject. Ironically, it has always been a non-Israelite and non-Jewish story. The land Job lived in was classically identified as Edom, Syria, Turkey, or even Oman, but never Israel, Judea, or Samaria. The story of Job is a Canaanite story, and much older than the rest of the Septuagint.

The original core of this story appears to have been a debate between Job and his three friends about which god to worship, not 'why does bad stuff happen to good people?' as many Jews and Christians glean from it today. The answer to that question would apparently be 'because the Lord lets the slanderer do evil stuff to good people.' The redacted texts in the Septuagint and Masoretic Text still contain many comparisons between the Lord and God (El), or the Lord and the Omnipotent

(Shaddai). El was the name of the supreme god in the Canaanite pantheon, however, the book of Job clearly describes a talking thundercloud hovering before Job, which is a description of Hadad, the god of thunder in the Canaanite religion. As some Israelites, such as the prophet Ezekiel, worshiped Ba'al Hadad, this text may have been used by the Judeans and Samaritans who worshiped Ba'al between 1000 and 600 BC, who are repeatedly mentioned in the books of Kingdoms (Masoretic Samuel and Kings) and Paralipomenons (Masoretic Divrê Hayyāmîm).

The book is clearly missing a great deal, including whatever the original conclusion was, and descriptions of the battle between the Lord and Leviathan (or Lotan), however, based on the similarities of the descriptions in the Ugaritic Texts from the 1200s BC, and the Apocalypse of John from around 100 AD, some version of the battle seems to have continued in use until the Christian Era. The Apocalypse of John not only included the seven-headed serpentine dragon being thrown out of the sky but also a description of a lion-beast like the Nemean lion, the brother of Ladon, the ancient Greek version of Lotan.

In 200 BC, the Greek Kingdom of Syria under the Seleucid Dynasty took Judea from Egypt and began an effort to Hellenize the Judeans, which included erecting a statue of Zeus in the Second Temple in Jerusalem and effectively banning traditional Judaism. This Hellenizing activity was partially successful, creating the Sadducee faction of Judaism, however, it also led to the Maccabean Revolt in 165 BC, which itself created the independent Kingdom of Judea in 140 BC. This Kingdom had a tenuous alliance with the Roman Republic until General Pompey conquered Syria for the Roman Republic in 69 BC. Pomey's goal was to liberate Greek-speaking communities in the Middle East that had fallen under the rule of non-Greeks when the Seleucid's Syrian Empire had collapsed, and he carved up Judea, and Edom to the southeast, placing Greek-speaking cities under the protection of the Roman province of Syria. He also liberated several smaller communities that had been occupied by Judea, granting them self-government, including Ashdod, Yavne, Jaffa, Dora, Marissa, and Samaria.

A series of wars including both Julius Caesar's campaigns, and a Parthian invasion led to the weakening of the Hasmonean dynasty, and in 37 AD, the Roman Senate appointed Herod the Great as King of the Judeans. Herod's rule wasn't particularly popular, as he allowed the Romans to establish themselves within Judea, however, he did expand Judea, reintegrating the Greek and Samaritan cities, and annexing Galilee and Edom.

When he died, his kingdom was divided between four successors, a situation that ended in 66 AD when the Romans conquered the region. An uprising in 120 AD led to the Jews being exiled from Judea, and the region became a Greco-Roman colony. In the wake of the Jews, the Samaritans rose in numbers, along with the Christians once Christianity was legalized. Between 529 and 555 AD, the Samaritans revolted and were effectively annihilated, by the Byzantine Empire.

Outside of Judea, the Septuagint was the dominant form of Jewish scriptures across the Greek-speaking world, which by the beginning of the Christian era extended from the Roman Empire in the west, to the Indo-Greek Kingdom in the east. Jewish traders had established small colonies along the trade routes of the Red Sea and the Indian Ocean, reaching as far south as Eritrea, and as far east as southern India, and these Jews spoke Greek and used the Septuagint. Daniel appears to have added to the Masoretic Text as a reference for Rabbis, as the Christians seemed so interested in the book. It was never fully translated into Hebrew and was acknowledged throughout Rabbinic Jewish history as being largely about astrology, which was considered a science in the dominantly Christian and Islamic nations until the Renaissance.

The earliest Christian Bibles, all used the Septuagint, however, by the 4th century some Christian scholars were debating whether they should retranslate the Old Testament from the version the Jews were using, and some even suggested using the Samaritan version. Both suggestions were generally dismissed as heretical, as Jesus and the Apostles had quoted from the Septuagint, even though they had access to the Hebrew version then in use. The Book of Daniel was the exception, as Theodotion's translation had supplanted the Old Greek translation by the 4th century. In the Middle Ages, the Latin Catholic Bibles eventually switched to the Masoretic text after the schism with the Orthodox Church in Byzantine.

In the east, Orthodox Bibles continued to use the Septuagint, as they do today. To the south, the Ethiopian Tewahedo Church continued to use the Septuagint, and across Asia, the Thomas Christians and Nestorians continued to use the Septuagint. Only in Western Europe were the later Masoretic Text adopted, abandoning the more ancient Septuagint, on the assumption that the Jews had copied their texts more faithfully than the Greeks had translated them. This assumption was carried forward into the Protestant Churches that broke off from the Catholic Church, and therefore almost all

Protestant Bibles use the Masoretic Text for the basis of the Old Testament.

Unfortunately, this means that the earliest Christian writing is generally confusing and ignored by Protestants and Catholics. The earliest Christians of the first and second centuries quoted books that are no longer in the Bible, and as such, their writings are not always understood. Septuagint: Job is a 21st century translation aimed at correcting this problem.

One of the problems with academic translations of the Septuagint is the use of unfamiliar names or terms, as the Septuagint was written in Greek, and therefore many names are unrecognizable to modern English readers who are used to Hebrew-derived names. This project uses the more commonly understood Hebrew-derived names instead of their Greek translations, such as Canaan instead of Chanaan, and Melchizedek instead of Melchisedec. Common modern names are also used instead of either Greek or Hebrew terms when geographical locations are known, such as the archaeological name Uruk instead of the Greek Orech, or the Hebrew Erech, and the archaeological term Sumer instead of Shinar or Senar. While this could be argued as not being a correct academic procedure, it does fulfill the goal of making the translation easy to read and understand.

Chapter 1

There was a certain man in the land of Aysitidi[1] whose name was Job,[2] and he was honest, blameless, lawful, god-respecting,[3] and abstained from all evil things. He had seven sons and three daughters. His livestock consisted of seven thousand sheep, three thousand camels, five hundred yoked oxen, five hundred donkeys in the pastures, and a very great household. He had the greatest herds on the earth, and he was a noble person of the eastern ancestors.[4]

His sons visited one another and prepared a banquet every day, including with them also their three sisters, to eat and drink with them. When the days of the banquet were completed, Job sent and purified them, having risen up in the morning, and offered sacrifices for them, according to their number, and one calf for a sin-offering for their minds, as Job thought, 'In case perhaps my sons have thought evil in their thoughts against God.'[5] This Job did continually.

It happened one day, that the messengers of God[6] came to stand before the Lord,[7] and the slanderer[8] came with them. The Lord asked the slanderer, "Where do you come from?"

The slanderer answered the Lord, "I have come from circling the Earth, and walking around in the world."

CHAPTER 1

The Lord said to him, "Have you diligently considered my servant Job, that there are none like him on the Earth, a man blameless, honest, god-respecting, abstaining from everything evil?"

The slanderer answered the Lord, "Does Job worship God for no reason? Have you not set a protection about him, and about his household, and all his possessions? Have you not blessed the works of his hands, and multiplied his livestock on the land? Put out your hand, and touch all that he has, and see if he will bless you to your face."

The Lord said to the slanderer, "Look, I'll give into your hands all that he has, but don't touch him," and the slanderer left the presence of the Lord.

It happened one day, that Job's sons and daughters were drinking wine in the house of their elder brother when a messenger came to Job, and said, "The yokes of oxen were plowing, and the jenny-donkeys were feeding near them when plunderers came and stole them and murdered your servants with their swords. I am the only one who escaped and have come to tell you."

While he was still speaking, another messenger came and said to Job, "Fire has fallen from the sky, and burned up the sheep along with the shepherds. I am the only one who escaped and have come to tell you."

While he was still speaking, another messenger came and said to Job, "Three bands of horsemen came against us, and surrounded and captured our camels, and killed your servants by the sword. I am the only one who escaped and have come to tell you."

While he was still speaking, another messenger came and said to Job, "While your sons and your daughters were eating and drinking with their elder brother, suddenly a great wind came in from the desert and lifted the four corners of the house, and the house fell on your children, and they are dead. I am the only one who escaped and have come to tell you."

Job rose and tore his garments. He shaved the hair off his head, fell to the ground, worshiped, and said, "I came out naked from my mother's womb, and naked will I return there. The Lord gave, and the Lord has taken away. As it seems good to the Lord, so it happens. Blessed be the name of the Lord."

In all these events that befell him, Job did not sin at all before the Lord and did not foolishly blame God.

CHAPTER 1

Chapter 1 Notes

1 Codex Vaticanus: Aysitidi (ᴀᵧϲιτιᴅι)

* Aleppo Codex: årṣ ôûṣ (אֶרֶץ עוּץ). Translation: land of Ous

* Leningrad Codex: eretz-utz (אֶרֶץ־עוּץ). Translation: land of Utz

* Targum to Job: årôāå deôûṣ (אַרְעָא דְעוּץ). Translation: land of Ous

The name of the land is also Aysitidi (Αυσίτιδι) in the Testaments of Job. The beginning of the name, Ays (αυσ), is a transliteration of the same term found in the Hebrew translation, while the rest of the word, itidi (ίτιδι), appears to be a transliteration of the cuneiform term itiatu (𒂊𒋛𒀀𒋾), meaning boundaries, environs, or region. This suggests the Aramaic version of Job was translated from a cuneiform source text.

The land of Aysitidi (or Ouz) was traditionally located by Biblical scholars somewhere in the periphery of Arabia and Edom (modern Jordan and southern Israel) or the periphery of Arabia and Syria (modern southern Syria). Several towns across Israel, Gaza, the West Bank, Syria, Lebanon, and even Oman have historical claims to be the "city of Job," and many "Tombs of Job" exist in these countries. The earliest known claim for the "City of Job" was Karnein in Syria which was recognized by Eusebius, in the 4th century as being the hometown of Job. Karnein is believed to have been in Bashan, southern Syria. According to one of the Dead Sea Scrolls referred to as the War Scroll, Ouz was on the other side of the Euphrates, placing it in Upper Mesopotamia.

CHAPTER 1

2 Codex Vaticanus: Iôb (ιⲟꞬⲃ)

- Dead Sea Scroll 4QpaleoJob^c (in chapter 13): Åyb (איוב)
- Aleppo Codex: âyûb (אֵיוֹב)
- Leningrad Codex: iyyov (אִיּוֹב)
- Vetus Latina manuscipts: Iob
- Targum to Job: âîôb (אִיוֹב)

The name "Job" was used in the region of Canaan since at least the time of the Amarna Letters, in which the name was transliterated into Akkadian Cuneiform as Ahiáab (𒀀𒄿𒀜), which was pronounced almost identical to the Hebrew Iyyov (אִיּוֹב) and Arabic Ayyub (أيوب).

3 Codex Vaticanus: dicaeos theosebês (ⲆⲓⲔⲀⲒⲞⲤⲐⲈⲞⲤⲈⲂⲎⲤ).

Translation: righteous (or observant, balanced, lawful) god-respecting (or devout, pious)

- Minuscule 205 (LXX 68): dicaeos alêthinos theosebês (ⲆⲓⲕⲀⲓⲟⲥ ⲁⲗⲏⲑⲓⲛⲟ̅ⲥ θⲉⲟⲥⲟⲃⲩⲗⲩⲥ). Translation: righteous (or observant, balanced, lawful) genuine (or trustworthy) god-respecting (or devout, pious)
- Aleppo Codex: ûyrå ålhym (וירא אלהים). Translation: respecting (or fearful of, revering, in awe of) goddesses (in Hebrew, or gods in Aramaic, or god in Assyrian and Babylonian, or Highest in Old Akkadian)
- Leningrad Codex: vire elohim (וַיִּרָא אֱלֹהִים). Translation: respecting (or fearful of, revering, in awe of) goddesses (in Hebrew, or gods in Aramaic, or god in Assyrian and Babylonian, or Highest in Old Akkadian)

CHAPTER 1

• Targum to Job: yya (?). Translation: Yhŭ

Ålhym (ᵔ᷈᷉ᐢᐢ) is the Aramaic word for 'gods,' and was occasionally translated that way in the Septuagint, such as when referring to the elohim of Egypt. The Hebrew word ålhym (אלהים) translates properly as 'goddesses,' however, it is also commonly accepted as a gender-neutral term meaning 'deities' due to its use as the word for 'gods' in the Masoretic text.

The problem with the word ålhym is that while it does not mean 'God' in a phonetic sense, it is generally translated that way in the Septuagint, and accepted as meaning 'God' by Jews and Christians. In many sentences where the word is used, it is clear from the context that a singular deity is being referenced, meaning that the Hebrew translators saw the Aramaic word as a proper name and simply transliterated it into Hebrew.

The terms ålhym (ᐯᙆᐱᐧᐟ) and ålhym (ᵔ᷈᷉ᐢᐢ), are also direct transcriptions of the Neo-Assyrian word elium (𒀭𒂊𒇽𒌝), which by the Iron Age meant 'god,' indicating that text had previously been written in cuneiform, and was translated into Aramaic or Phoenician during the Iron Age. During the bronze age, the word alium (𒀭𒈨𒂊𒇽𒌝) referred to a specific god, [deity]Ān (𒀭𒀭) the highest god, and father of the other gods. His Akkadian name was derived from the word elûm (𒂊𒇻𒈨), meaning "higher," as the term was intended to convey the meaning of "highest." He was believed to live in the polar region of the sky, where the modern constellation of Draco is located, making him the highest in the sky, around which all the gods (stars) circled.

CHAPTER 1

During the Old Babylonian and Old Assyrian eras, the gods Marduk and Ashur, the national gods of Babylon and Assyria, replaced the Akkadian Alium as the primary god of the Mesopotamian pantheons, and by the Iron Age, the word elium had come to mean "god," explaining why the Aramaic term âlhym (אלהים) would have been interpreted as "god," by the Greeks. This means that the origin of the first chapters of Cosmic Genesis would have to have been in the Sumerian or Akkadian era, before the emergence of the Old Babylonian empire, and that the form of Cuneiform it was written in before being translated into Aramaic and Canaanite was Old Akkadian.

4 Codex Vaticanus: anthrôpos ecinos eugenês tôn aph Êliou anatolôn (ΑΝΘΡΩΠΟC ΕΚΕΙΝΟC ΕΥΓΕΝΗC ΤΩΝ ΑΦ ΗΛΙΟΥ ΑΝΑΤΟΛΩΝ). Translation: person that is noble the from sun (or Helios, east, day) easterners

- Aleppo Codex: håyš hhůå gdůl mkl bny qdm (האיש ההוא גדול מכל בני קדם). Translation: the man that is big (or important) container (or tank) the easterners (or Aramaic: ancestors)

- Leningrad Codex: Ha'ish hahu gadovl mikkol-benei-kedem (הָאִישׁ הַהוּא גָּדוֹל מִכָּל־בְּנֵי־קֶדֶם). Translation: the man that big (or important) container (or tank) the easterners (or Aramaic: ancestors)

- Targum to Job: gabrå hahûå rab beniksîn mikkål benê madinhå (גַבְרָא הַהוּא רַב בְּנִכְסִין מִכָּל בְּנֵי מַדִנְחָא). Translation: man that is great (or fights, shoots) in (or with, for) prophecies container sons of the east

CHAPTER 1

Both the Greek and Hebrew translators seem to have had difficulties translating the Book of Job. In this case, combining the Greek, Hebrew, and Aramaic interpretations of the Hebrew words, results in "noble person of the eastern ancestors," however, it is possible that the text originally said he was an a "important prophet among the easterners."

5 Codex Vaticanus: theon (ΘЄΟΝ). Translation: god (or God)

- Aleppo Codex: ålhym (אלהים). Translation: goddesses (in Hebrew, or gods in Aramaic, or god in Assyrian and Babylonian, or Highest in Old Akkadian)
- Leningrad Codex: elohim (אֱלֹהִים). Translation: goddesses (in Hebrew, or gods in Aramaic, or god in Assyrian and Babylonian, or Highest in Old Akkadian)
- Targum to Job: dāḥēl min qŏdām yeyā (דְחֵל מִן קֳדָם יְיָ). Translation: fear from before Yhů

6 Codex Vaticanus: angeloe tou theou (ΑΓΓΕΛΟΙ ΤΟΥ ΘЄΟΥ). Translation: messengers (or angels) the god

- Aleppo Codex: bny hålhym (בני האלהים). Translation: sons (or decedents) the goddesses (in Hebrew, or 'the gods' in Aramaic, or 'the god' in Assyrian and Babylonian, or 'the Highest' in Old Akkadian)
- Leningrad Codex: benei ha'elohim (בְּנֵי הָאֱלֹהִים). Translation: sons (or decedents) the goddesses (in Hebrew, or 'the gods' in Aramaic, or 'the god' in Assyrian and Babylonian, or 'the Highest' in Old Akkadian)

40

CHAPTER 1

- Targum to Job: mal'achaya (מַלְאָכַיָא). Translation: angels (or messengers)

The term used in the Masoretic version of Job was also used in Bereshít (Masoretic Cosmic Genesis), where it was translated as 'sons of the God' (ΥΙΟΙΤΟΥΘΕΟΥ) in the Codex Cottonianus and 'messengers of the God' (ΑΓΓΕΛΟΙ ΤΟΥ ΘΕΟΥ) in the Codex Alexandrinus. They were also called Ôyryn (ОРᲜᲝᲠᲘ), meaning 'watchers' or 'guardians' in the Books of Enoch and Grigori (ⴆხፇⴆჳხፇ) in the Secrets of Enoch, likely transliterated from the Greek egirô (ἐγείρω) meaning 'awaken.' Given the similarity of the stories and the connections to Mount Hermon, they were likely based on the older Akkadian Igigi (𒂊𒅅𒈨𒅅𒈨), a group of lesser gods that rebelled against the ruling ᵃⁿAnuna (𒀭𒈨𒂗𒆠). The name ᵃⁿAnuna translates as 'sons of ᵈᵉⁱᵗʸĀn/sky' in Akkadian, suggesting this term was AnAnuna in Cuneiform. The ᵃⁿAnuna were a group of ruling gods, conceptually similar to the Olympian gods of Greek mythology. Significant members of this group of gods include ᵃⁿEnki (𒀭𒂗𒆠) the god of earth (or soil), and ᵃⁿEnlil (𒀭𒂗𒆤) the god of spirit who made the first humans in Mesopotamian beliefs. They were also called the ᵃⁿAnunakene (𒀭𒈨𒂗𒀀𒆤), more commonly transliterated into English as Anunnaki, as they described as being the 'children of An (the sky god) on Ki (the Earth).

CHAPTER 1

7 Codex Vaticanus: cyriou (ΚΥΡΙΟΥ). Translation: lord (or master, owner)

- Codex Sinaiticus: cyriou theoi (ΚΥΡΙΟΥΘΕΟΥ).

Translation: lord (or master, owner) God

- Aleppo Codex: yhůh (יהוה)
- Leningrad Codex: yehvah (יְהוָה)
- Targum to Job: yeyā (יְיָ). Translation: Yhů

8 Codex Vaticanus: diabolô (ⲇⲓⲁⲃⲟⲗⲱ). Translation: devil (or slanderer)

- Septuagint manuscript 406: diabolon (ⲇⲓⲁⲙⲟⲗⲟⲛ).

Translation: devil (or slanderer)

- Aleppo Codex: hšṭn (השטן). Translation: the adversary (or devil, opponent, Satan)
- Leningrad Codex: hassatan (הַשָּׂטָן). Translation: the adversary (or devil, opponent, Satan)
- Targum to Job: siṭnā (סְטָנָא). Translation: adversary (or opponent, Satan)

The term is documented in Aramaic as stnå (אׁטׂג), meaning adversary or devil, however, like the term "Lord," the adversary remains unnamed in the text. As the concept of the "devil" did not exist in Greek beliefs when the text was translated, the translator likely intended the term to be treated as 'slanderer,' and not "devil."

Chapter 2

It happened one day, that the angels of God came to stand before the Lord, and the slanderer came with them to stand before the Lord.

The Lord asked the slanderer, "Where had you come from?"

The slanderer answered the Lord, "I have come from traveling through the world, and wandering about the whole Earth."

The Lord asked the slanderer, "Have you then seen my servant Job, that there is no one among men on the Earth like him, a harmless, true, blameless, godly man, abstaining from all evil? He still clings to innocence, even after you have told me to destroy his property without reason?"

The slanderer answered the Lord, "Skin for skin. All that a man has will he give as a ransom for his life. No! Put out your hand, and touch his bones and his flesh, and see if he will bless you to your face."

The Lord said to the slanderer, "I give him over to you. Only spare his life."

So the slanderer left the Lord and infected Job with sore boils from his feet to his head. He took a potsherd to scrape away the discharge and sat on a dung heap outside the city.

After a lot of time had passed, his wife asked him, "How long will you hold out, saying, 'I wait yet a little while, expecting the hope of my deliverance?' Your descendants are abolished from the Earth, including your sons and daughters who with the labor and pains of my womb which I carried in vain with sorrows, and you yourself sit down to spend the nights in the open air among the corruption of worms, and I am a vagabond and a servant wandering from place to place and house to house, waiting for the setting of the sun, that I may rest from my labor and my struggles which now trouble me. Just say something against the Lord, and die."

He looked at her, and said to her, "You speak like a foolish woman. If we have received good things from the hand of the Lord, will we not survive evil things?"

In all these things that happened to him, Job did not sin at all with his lips before God. Now his three friends had heard of all the evil that had come upon him and came to him each from his own country, Eliphaz[1] the Temanite king,[2] Bildad the Shuhite tyrant,[3] and Zophar the Minaean king.[4] They came to him together, to visit and comfort him. When they saw him from a distance they did not know him, and they cried loudly and wept, and everyone ripped his clothing and threw dirt on his head. They sat down beside him seven days and seven nights, and not one of them spoke, as they saw that his disease was dreadful.

Chapter 2 Notes

1 Codex Vaticanus: Eliphaz (ελειφλz)
* Codex Sinaiticus: Eliphas (ελιφλc)
* Septuagint manuscript 620: Eliphatz (Ϭλιϸλτz)

* Aleppo Codex: Ålypz (אליפז)
* Leningrad Codex: Elifaz (אֱלִיפַז)
* Bohairic manuscripts: Elisaph (Ελιcαφ)
* Targum to Job: Elifaz (אֱלִיפַז)

The Hebrew name translates approximately as 'god is beautiful.' This could be the same Eliphaz as in Exodus, chapter 17, who was the firstborn son of Esau, or a different person with the same name. Based on the fact that he is called the King of Teman, it seems likely it was intended to be the same person, as Teman was an Edomite clan, and the Edomites were descendants of Esau according to the book of Deuteronomy, chapter 25. If the Eliphaz that visited Job was Esau's son, then this would place the life of Job around the same time as the life of Joseph and the rest of the twelve patriarchs. The traditional dating for Joseph's life is anywhere between 1800 and 1200 BC, which would correspond with the reference in the Song of Eliphaz from the Testament of Job to the North Star as being in Draco, which it has not been since the second millennium BC.

2 Codex Vaticanus: Thaemanôn basileus (ⲐⲀⲒⲘⲀⲚⲰⲚ ⲂⲀⳠⲒⲀⲈⳘⳠⲥ). Translation: Temanite king (or chief, master, lord, patron)

* Codex Alexandrinus: Themanôn basileus (ⲐⲈⲘⲀⲚⲰⲚ ⲂⲀⳠⲒⲀⲈⳘⳠⲥ). Translation: Temanite king (or chief, master, lord, patron)
* Aleppo Codex: tymny (תימני). Translation: southerner (Temanite, Yemenite)
* Leningrad Codex: teimani (תֵּימָנִי). Translation: southerner (Temanite, Yemenite)
* Targum to Job: dî min têmān (דִּי מִן תֵּימָן). Translation: who was from Teman

Teman (תימן) was both the name of a clan and a town in Edom (Idumea) in the time of ancient Judea. The Temanites were reported to be the descendants of Eliphaz, the son of Esau in the Torah's book of Exodus in chapter 17, and Deuteronomy in chapter 25. Based on the Greek reference to Eliphaz being the Temanite patron (or king), it seems likely the Creek translators viewed this Eliphaz as being Esau's son. The Hebrew translation could be interpreted in various ways, including that Eliphaz was simply a 'southerner,' meaning an Arab in general.

3 Codex Vaticanus: Baldad o Sauchaeôn tyrannos (ⲂⲀⲖⲆⲀⲆ ⲟⲤⲀⳘⲬⲀⲒⲰⲚⲦⳘⲢⲀⲚⲚⲟⲥ). Translation: Baldad the Shuhite tyrant

* Codex Alexandrinus: Baldas o Auchaeôn tyrannos (ⲂⲀⲖⲆⲀⲤⲟⲀⳘⲬⲀⲒⲰⲚⲦⳘⲢⲀⲚⲚⲟⲥ). Translation: Baldas the Achaean tyrant

- Miniscule 205 (LXX 68): Beldad o Saucheôn tyrannos (ϐϬλαλα ο cλυχλιοον τυβαννοσ). Translation: Beldad the Shuhite tyrant
- Septuagint manuscript 137: Aldad o Sauchaeôn tyrannos (Αλαλα ο cλυχλιοον τυβαννοσ). Translation: Aldad the Shuhite tyrant
- Septuagint manuscript 252: Baldad o Saucheôn tyrannos (ϐαλαλα ο cλυχϬοον τυβαννοσ). Translation: Baldad the Shuhite tyrant
- Septuagint manuscript 339: Baldad o Sauchiôn tyrannos (ϐαλαλα ο cλυχιοον τυβαννοσ). Translation: Baldad the Shuhite tyrant
- Aleppo Codex: bldd hšûḥy (בלדד השוחי). Translation: Bildad the Shuhite
- Leningrad Codex: vildad hashuchi (בִּלְדַּד הַשּׁוּחִי). Translation: Bildad the Shuhite
- Targum to Job: bildad dî min šûaḥ (בְּלְדַד דִּי מִן שׁוּחַ). Translation: Bildad who was from Shuah

According to the Torah, the Shuhites were descendants of Abraham's son Shuah. According to Neshite (Hittite) records, the Shuhites lived in northern modern Syria on the Euphrates River, south of the Hittite capital of Carchemish.

4 Codex Vaticanus: Sôphar o Minaeôn basileus (cωϕαρ ο μειναιων βαϲιλεYc). Translation: Sôphar the Minaean king

CHAPTER 2

- Codex Alexandrinus: Sôphar o Minaeôn basileus (ⲥⲱⲫⲁⲣ
ⲟ ⲘⲒⲚⲀⲒⲱⲚ ⲂⲀⲥⲒⲗⲉⲨⲥ). Translation: Sôphar the Minaean
king
- Codex Ephraemi Rescriptus (LXX C): Sôphar o Minnaeôn
basileus (ⲥⲱⲫⲁⲣ ⲟ ⲘⲒⲚⲚⲀⲒⲱⲚ ⲂⲀⲥⲒⲗⲉⲨⲥ). Translation:
Sôphar the Minaean king
- Septuagint manuscript 249: Sôphar ho Mênaeôn basileus
(σωϕⲁβ̌ ο μⲓⲱ̄ⲛ̄ⲇⲓⲟⲟⲛ ⲩⲇⲥⲓⲗⲋ̄ⲕ̄ⲥ). Translation: Sôphar the
Minaean king
- Septuagint manuscript 261: Sôphar ho Minnaeos basileus
(σωϕⲁβ̌ ο μⲛ̄ⲛ̄ⲇⲓⲟⲥ ⲩⲇⲥⲓⲗⲋ̄ⲕ̄ⲥ). Translation: Sôphar the Minaean
king
- Septuagint manuscript 575: Sophar o Minaeôn basileus
(σωϕⲁβ̌ ο μⲛ̄ⲇϥ̄ⲟⲟⲛ ⲩⲇⲥⲓⲗⲋ̄ⲕ̄ⲥ). Translation: Sophar the Minaean
king
- Septuagint manuscript 728: Sôphar ho Mêniaeôn basileus
(σωϕⲁβ̌ ο μⲓⲱ̄ⲛ̄ⲓⲇⲓⲟⲟⲛ ⲩⲇⲥⲓⲗⲋ̄ⲕ̄ⲥ). Translation: Sôphar the
Minaean king
- Septuagint manuscript 975: Sôphar ho Mênnaeôn basileus
(σωϕⲁβ̌ ο μⲓⲱ̄ⲛ̄ⲛ̄ⲇⲓⲟⲟⲛ ⲩⲇⲥⲓⲗⲋ̄ⲕ̄ⲥ). Translation: Sôphar the
Minaean king
- Aleppo Codex: sûpr hnômty (צוֹפַר הנעמתי). Translation:
Sûpr the Naamathite
- Leningrad Codex: tzovfar hanna'amati (צוֹפַר הַנַּעֲמָתִי).
Translation: Tzovfar the Naamathite
- Sahidic manuscripts: Meinnaiôn (ⲘⲉⲒⲚⲚⲀⲒⲱⲚ)
- Bohairic manuscripts: Minneôn (ⲘⲒⲚⲚⲉⲱⲚ)

48

• Targum to Job: ṣôpar dî min naôămâ (צוֹפַר דִּי מִן נַעֲמָה).

Translation: Zopar who was from Naamah

The Septuagint and Masoretic texts use different terms in this verse and refer to lands that were quite distant from each other. It is unclear which term was originally used, and it is possible that neither term is the original as the oldest fragments found among the Dead Sea Scrolls are written in Canaanite (Judahite, Edomite, or Samaritan). The reason for the two different terms is likely because both the Greek and Hebrew texts were translated from Canaanite, however, the Book of Job appears to have never been important to the surviving Samaritan community, and therefore this text likely originates with a different group using the Canaanite script, such as the Edomites. Given the time period referenced by the Thuban as the North Star in the Song of Eliphaz in the Testament of Job, the story was set during the time before the Israelites invaded Canaan, and therefore it was likely a Canaanite story that was adopted by the Israelites at some point.

The Minaeans were the people of the Kingdom of Ma'in in modern Yemen. They appeared in several ancient Greek works, including the works of Eratosthenes, as well as the Septuagint's 2nd Paralipomenon, chapter 20 where they were in an alliance against King Jehoshaphat. The region of Ma'in appears to have been part of the Kingdom of Saba until after 400 BC, and, therefore, if the Minaeans were mentioned in the original Canaanite book of Job, this would be a reference to a Saban group.

CHAPTER 2

The Aleppo Codex substitutes the word nômty (נעמתי) which is generally translated as Naamathites, who were the people from the ancient Canaanite city of Naamah. The city of Naamah was listed as one of the towns conquered by Joshua and resettled by the Israelites in the Book of Joshua, which, if Naamah was the original term used in the text, places the story of Job before the time of Joshua.

Chapter 3

After this, Job opened his mouth and cursed his days, saying, "If only I'd have died in the day I was born," and of that night he said, "Let that night be darkness, and don't let the Lord see it from above, or let the light have shone on it. Let darkness and the shadow of Mot[1] seize it, and let blackness come on it. Let that day and night be cursed, let darkness carry it away. Don't let it be counted among the days of the year, or within the days of the months. Let that night be pain, and don't let happiness or joy come on it. Let he who curses the day curse it, including he who is ready to attack the Great Cetus,[2] and let the stars of that night be darkened, and let them remain dark, and not return to the light. Let it not see the rising of Shahar,[3] because it did not shut up the gates of my mother's womb because if it did, it would have removed sorrow from my eyes."

"Why didn't I die in the belly? Why did I not come out from the womb and die immediately? Why did the knees support me? Why did I suck the breasts? Now I should have lain down and been quiet, I should have slept and been at rest, with kings and councilors of the earth, who praised their swords, or with rulers, whose gold was abundant, and who filled their houses with silver, or I should have been as an untimely birth proceeding from his mother's womb, or as infants who never saw light.

There the ungodly have burnt out the fury of rage, there the wearied in body rest. The men of old times have together ceased to hear the exactor's voice. The small and great are there, and the servant that was afraid of his lord. Why is light given to those who are in bitterness, and life to those minds who are in grief? Who desires death, and does not obtain it, digging for it as for treasures, and would be very joyful if they should gain it? Death is rest to such a man, for God has hedged him in. For my groaning comes before my food, and I cry beset with terror. The terror of which I meditated has come over me, and that which I was afraid of has happened to me. I was not at peace, nor quiet, nor had I rest, yet anger came on me.

Chapter 3 Notes

1 Codex Vaticanus: Thanatou (ΘΑΝΑΤΟΥ). Translation: Thanatos (or death, corpse)

- Aleppo Codex: mût (מות). Translation: Mot (or death)
- Leningrad Codex: mavet (מָוֶת). Translation: Mot (or death)
- Targum to Job: môtå (מוֹתָא). Translation: Zopar who was from Naamah

Mot was the ancient Canaanite god of death, known as Mt (𐎄—) in Ugaritic Canaanite during the Late Bronze Age, and Mt (𐤋𐤏) in Phoenician Canaanite during the Iron Age. He was interpreted as the Israelite messenger (angel) of death in the Classical Era. Thanatos was an ancient Greek god of death and the early Christian angel of death.

2 Codex Vaticanus: mega cêtos (ΜΕΓΑΚΗΤΟΟ). Translation: great Cetus (or whale, sea monster)

- Aleppo Codex: lûytn (לֹוִיתָן)
- Leningrad Codex: livyatan (לִוְיָתָ֔ן)
- Targum to Job: âlyûtehôn (אֱלְיוּתְהוֹן)

The Great Cetus refers to the constellation Cetus, which was known as the asterism Lôtān (𒁹— ⟶) Ugaritic Canaanite during the Late Bronze Age, and in Lûtān (𐤋𐤈𐤍) in Phoenician Canaanite during the Iron Age.

The Greek name Cetus (Κῆτος) is generally associated with the myth of Perseus, where the demigod Perseus traveled to Aethiopia to kill Cetus in order to rescue the Princess Andromeda. The Cetus is also mentioned in Genesis and implied in the Psalms.

The term Leviathan is also translated as "dragon" (δράκων) in the Septuagint, which is also the term that tanninim (תַּנִּינָם) was translated as in Hebrew, implying the Hebrew translators were apprehensive about translating the name Leviathan, or Leviathan was the name of the dragon (תַּנִּינָם). The term Leviathan was used in the book of Isaiah, in a quote from the Ugaritic Texts which substituted the name Leviathan for Lotan, the ancient Canaanite sea monster described as having seven heads. The name Lotan is accepted as the source of the Greek myth of Ladon, the serpent-like dragon that twisted around the tree in the Garden of the Hesperides and guarded the golden apples. This means that

Lotan / Leviathan may have been the name of the serpent-like dragon in an earlier rendition of the Garden of Eden story. However, in this case, Job is referring to the constellation Cetus, as is evident from the reference to the stars being darkened.

3 Codex Vaticanus: eôsphoron anatellonta (ЄѡϹΦΟΡΟΝ ΑΝΑΤΕΛΛΟΝΤΑ). Translation: Heosphorus rising

- Aleppo Codex: bôpôpy šhr (בעפעפי שחר). Translation: waking (or opening eyelids) of Shahar (or dawn)
- Leningrad Codex: be'af'appei-shachar (בְּעַפְעַפֵּי־שָׁחַר). Translation: waking (or opening eyelids) of Shahar (or dawn)
- Targum to Job: betîmôrê qeraṣtå (בְּתִימוֹרֵי קְרַצְתָּא). Translation: house of fear in the early

Eosphorus was a Greek name for the planet Venus as the morning star, the equivalent of the Roman morning star god Lucifer. The Canaanite equivalent of Heosphorus was Helel (הֵילֵל) the son of Shahar (Helel ben Shahar), not Shahar, indicating that the Canaanite text the Greeks translated from was slightly different from the text the Hebrew translators worked from.

Chapter 4

Then Eliphaz the Temanite asked, "Have you often spoken in such distress? Who will endure the force of your words? You have instructed many, and have strengthened the hands of the weak ones, and have supported the sick with words, and have imparted courage to weak knees. Yet, now that pain has come on you, and touched you, you are troubled. Is your fear not founded in foolishness? Your hope also, and the mischief of your ways? Remember, who has perished being pure? When were the honest-hearted completely destroyed? Accordingly, as I have seen men plowing barren places, and they that sow them will reap sorrows for themselves. They will perish by the command of the Lord and will be completely consumed by the breath of his anger. The strength of the lion, the voice of the lioness, and the exulting cry of lion cubs are quenched. The old lion has perished for lack of food, and the lions' cubs have forgotten one another. But if there had been any truth in your words, none of these evils would have happened to you."

"Will my ear not receive excellent revelations from him? When terror falls on men, with dread and sound in the night, horror and trembling seized me, and caused all my bones greatly to shake. A wind[1] came against my face, and my hair and skin shivered. I rose but could not see it, I looked, and there, was nothing before my eyes, but I still heard a breath and a voice, saying, 'What? Will a mortal be pure before the Lord, or a man blameless regarding his work, when he doesn't trust his servants and sees perversion in his angels? As for those that live in houses of clay, the same clay we are formed from, he kills them like a moth. From morning to evening they no longer exist, they have died because they can't help themselves. He blows on them, and they are withered, they have died for lack of wisdom.'"

Chapter 4 Notes

1 Codex Vaticanus: pneuma (ⲡⲛⲉⲩⲙⲁ). Translation: wind (or spirit, breath, ghost)

• Aleppo Codex: rûḥ (רוח). Translation: wind (or spirit, breath, ghost)

• Leningrad Codex: ruach (רוּחַ). Translation: wind (or spirit, breath, ghost)

• Targum to Job: zîqå (זיקא). Translation: blast (or shooting star, wind, comet, draft)

Chapter 5

[Eliphaz continued,] "Call, if anyone will listen to you, or if you will see any of the sacred messengers. Anger destroys the foolish one, and envy kills him who has gone astray. I have seen foolish ones taking root, but suddenly their home was devoured. Let their children be far from safety, and let them be crushed at the doors of vile men, and let there be no deliverer. For what they have collected, the just will eat, but they will not be delivered out of calamities. Let their strength be completely exhausted. For labor can't by any means come out of the Earth or will trouble spring out of the mountains. Yet man is born through labor, and the sons of Resheph[1] seek the heights."

"Nevertheless, I will beg the Lord and will call on the Lord, the sovereign of all. Who does great things and untraceable, glorious things also, and marvelous, of which there is no number? Who gives rain on the Earth, sending water on the earth? Who exalts the lowly, and raises up them that are lost, frustrating the counsel of the cunning, and their hands will not perform the truth? Who takes the wise in their wisdom, and subverts the counsel of the cunning in the day darkness will come on them, and let them grope in the noon-day even as in the night, and lets them perish in war, and lets the weak escape from the hand of the mighty?"

CHAPTER 5

"Let the weak have hope, but the mouth of the unjust be closed. Blessed is the man who the Lord has reproved and rejected, not the chosen of Resheph.[2] He causes a man to be in pain, and restores him again, he smites, and his hands heal. Six times he will deliver you out of distresses, and in the seventh harm will not touch you. In famine, he will deliver you from death, and in war, he will free you from the power of the sword. He will hide you from the scourge of the tongue, and you will not be afraid of coming evils."

"You will laugh at the unrighteous and the lawless, and you will not be afraid of wild beasts. For the wild beasts of the field will be at peace with you. Then you will know that your house will be at peace, and the provision for your tabernacle will not fail. You will know that your seed will be abundant, and your children will be like the plants of the field. You will come to the grave like ripe grain reaped in its season, or as a heap of the grain flour collected in proper time. Look, we have thus wanted out these matters, these are what we have heard, but you reflect on yourself and see if you have done anything wrong."

CHAPTER 5

Chapter 5 Notes

1 Codex Vaticanus: neossoe de gypos (ΝΕΟCCΟΙ ΔΕ ΓΥΠΟC). Translation: nestlings of the vulture

• Septuagint manuscript 252. νεοσσοε de gypôn (νόσοσοι Ἀσ́ γυπον). Translation: nestlings vulture

• Septuagint manuscript 705: neossoe gypos (νόσοσοι γυπος). Translation: nestlings vulture

• Aleppo Codex: bny-ršp (בני-רשף). Translation: sons of Resheph (or coals, flames, sparks, lightning, thunderbolts, arrows, heat, fever, plague)

• Leningrad Codex: venei-reshef (בְנֵי־רֶשֶׁף). Translation: sons of Resheph (or coals, flames, sparks, lightning, thunderbolts, arrows, heat, fever, plague)

• Targum to Job: zîqå (זִיקָא). Translation: blast (or shooting star, wind, comet, draft)

This line of text, along with others in the Septuagint that appear as rešep (רשף) in the Masoretic Text, has always been a source of debate, as the Greek translators did not know what rešep meant, and therefore translated it various ways, including 'vultures' in this verse. Jerome decided to not translate the word when he created the Vulgate Latin Bible in the 4th century, transcribing it as Rapha. This confusion reentered Catholic and Protestant Bibles when Luther and the others decided to translate the Old Testament from the Masoretic text, and therefore different translations of the Bible translated rešep as "sparks," "coals," or "vultures" (if simply substituting the Septuagint's translation). Since archaeological discoveries in the 1900s, it has become clear that Rešep (רשף) was a god, generally called Resheph or one of several variations, including Rahshaf, Rasap, Rashap, Resep, Reshef, Reshpu, Rapha, and Repheth.

Both the Ugaritic Canaanite spelling of the name, Ršp (𐎗𐎌𐎔) from the Late Bronze Age, and the Phoenician Canaanite spelling of the name, Ršp (𐤓𐤔𐤐) from the Iron Age, are identical to the Hebrew spelling found in the Aleppo Codex: Ršp (רשף), confirming that it is the name of the god. His name was spelled similarly in Eblaite as [deity]Rašap (𒀭𒊨𒀊), and in Egyptian as Ršpu (𓂋𓈙𓊪𓏤) in the Middle Bronze Age, as he had been worshiped in the region for a long time. The Old Babylonian version of Rasheph was Nergal, who was also known as Aplu Enlil, meaning the "son of Enlil." This Old Babylonian title became his Hurrian name, Aplu during the Middle Bronze Age, which itself became the Hittite version of the name, Āppaliunāš (𒀀𒀊𒉺𒇷𒌋𒈾𒀸) during the Late Bronze Age, which was adopted as by the Early Iron Age Greeks in Cyprus as Apeílōn (Ἀπείλων), and ultimately became the Greek god Apollo (Ἀπόλλων). Both Respeph and Apollo were described as shooting people with arrows of disease, which Job later refers to himself as having been shot with by the Lord, suggesting that Eliphaz was a Resheph worshiper.

As the Greek translators did not recognize the name Rešeph as being Apollo, they substituted something that did want to fly, the nestlings of a vulture, however, as the word is a proper name it is restored to Resheph in this translation.

2 Codex Vaticanus: pantocratoros (ΠΑΝΤΟΚΡΑΤΟΡΟϹ).
Translation: omnipotent

• Aleppo Codex: šdy (שׁדי). Translation: devilish (demonic, phantom)

• Leningrad Codex: šadday (שַׁדָּי). Translation: devilish (demonic, phantom)

• Targum to Job: šaday (שַׁדָּי). Translation: shooter (or diabolical, demonic, breast, almighty, field)

The Septuagint and Masoretic translations often differ in regards to the name or title Šdy, suggesting that the Aramaic and Canaanite (Judahite or Samaritan) source texts they worked from differed in regards to this word. The term was omitted throughout Cosmic Genesis, suggesting that when the word was first encountered the Greeks did not know how to interpret it, as Bereshít (Masoretic Cosmic Genesis) is the first book of the Torah, the first collection of Israelite texts probably translated at the Library of Alexandria. It is equally possible that it was the earlier Aramaic translator who had omitted it, however, it was almost certainly in the Canaanite version the translator worked from, as it is used consistently in Bereshít, and is mentioned again when Moses god's name Ôn is introduced in Exodus.

The confusion over the term šdy likely stems from the different meanings of the word in Canaanite and Aramaic. In Akkadian cuneiform, the term was [deity]šēdu (✳𐤄), referring to a "protective spirit" or "lesser god." Later in Aramaic, the word became šydå (𐡔𐡉𐡃𐡀), meaning "demon" in the classical sense, as a type of muse or nymph. Whereas in Canaanite, šdy (𐤔𐤃𐤉) took on a different meaning, generally interpreted as "powerful" by the Early Classical Era. This is likely where the Greeks derived the term "omnipotent" (παντοκράτοροσ), which was later used in the Septuagint where the Masoretic text generally uses the term šdy.

This alternate interpretation of the word šdy (𐤔𐤃𐤉) in Canaanite is likely due to the Egyptian New Kingdom era rule over Canaan. During the early New Kingdom era, the worship of Resheph was suppressed due to his association with the earlier Hyksos dynasty. In the early New Kingdom era, religious texts about Resheph would have been updated to Shed (𓆷𓂝𓏛, transliteration: šd), who was often referred to as "the savior," and was virtually identical to the earlier Canaanite god Resheph. This name would have been transliterated into Canaanite using the Cuneiform script in the late New Kingdom era as ᵈᵉⁱᵗʸšēdu (𒀭𒐐), before being translated into Canaanite using the Phoenician script in the early Iron Age as šdy (𐤔𐤃𐤉), resulting in the confusing identification of Resheph as a "demonic" (𐤔𐤉𐤃𐤀) god in Aramaic.

In the northern Canaan region, which was previously inhabited by the Amorites and later dominated by the Aramaic people, the Hurrians, who were under the rule of the Mitanni Empire, referred to a deity as Ablu (𒀊𒇻). This name is generally accepted as a shortened version of aplu ᶦˡᵘEllil (𒀊𒇻 𒀭𒂗𒆤), which is an epithet of Nergal, the son of the Old Babylonian god Ellil. Ablu, like Resheph and Nergal, was considered a god associated with both plague and healing. The worship of Ablu extended to the Neshite (Hittite) and Trojan civilizations, where he was known as the god Apaliunas (𒀳𒀸𒈾𒀸𒆠) as mentioned in a peace treaty between the civilizations in 1280 BC. Homer's Illiad reported that Apollôn (Απολλων) was the god who built the wall of Troy, confirming that the Greeks equated Apaliunas with Apollo.

In the Illiad, a priest of Apollo called Chryses, referred to Apollo as the "Lord of Mice" as he was believed to protect from plagues of mice. This suggests that the Pelesets viewed Shaddai as a version of Apaliunas when they captured the box of the covenant in 1st Kingdoms (Masoretic Samuel), as they returned it with golden statues of mice after their cities were plagued by swarms of mice.

The Masoretic Book of Job treats God and Shaddai as two separate beings. While this is not clear in the Septuagint's Book of Job, the alternative interpretation is that a god named Shaddai spends a lot of time talking to himself, and therefore this translation follows the Masoretic treatment of these gods. As the name Rasheph is already present in the Masoretic version of the chapter, and Shaddai is a descendant of that name, the older name Rasheph is used as a translation for "pantocratoros."

Chapter 6

Job answered and said, "If only that one would indeed weigh the anger that is on me, and take up my griefs in a balance them together! They would be heavier than the sand by the seashore, but, as it seems, my words are vain. For the arrows of the Lord are in my body, whose violence drinks up my blood. Whenever I speak, they pierce me. What then? Will the wild donkey bray for nothing, if he is not seeking food? Again, will the ox stay at the manger, when he has fodder? Will bread be eaten without salt? Again, is there taste in empty words? My anger can't cease, for I perceive my food as smelling like a stinking lion. If only he would grant my desire, and my petition might be heard, and the Lord would grant my hope! Let the Lord torture me, but don't let him completely destroy me! Let the grave be my city, on the walls of which I have leaped. I will not shrink from it, for I have not denied the sacred words of my God."

"What is my strength, that I continue? What is my time, that my mind endures? Is my strength the strength of stones? Is my flesh of brass? Have I not trusted in him? Yet help is far from me! Mercy has rejected me, and the visitors of the Lord have ignored me. My nearest relations have not regarded me, they have passed me by like a failing brook, or like a wave. They who used to reverence me, now have turned against me like snow or hardened ice. When it has melted at the approach of heat, it is not known what it was, and likewise, I have also been deserted by all, and I am ruined and have become an outcast. Look the ways of the Temanites, you that mark the paths of the Sabaeans?"[1]

"They that trust in cities and riches will come to shame as well. You have also come to me without pity so that seeing my wounds you are afraid. What? Have I made any demand of you? Do I ask for strength from you, to deliver me from enemies, or to rescue me from the hand of the mighty ones? Teach me, and I will be silent. If in anything I have erred, tell me. As it seems, the words of an honest man are vain, because I do not ask strength from you. Neither will your reproof cause me to cease my words, as I will not endure the sound of your speech. Even because you attack the fatherless, and insult your friend. Now, having looked at your countenances, I will not lie. Sit down now, and let there not be unrighteousness, and unite again with the just. For there is no injustice in my tongue, and does not my throat meditate understanding?"

Chapter 6 Notes

1 Codex Vaticanus: Sabôn (ⲥⲁⲃⲱⲛ). Translation: Sabeans

• Codex Sinaiticus: Esebôn (ⲉⲥⲉⲃⲱⲛ)

CHAPTER 6

- Codex Alexandrinus: asebôn (ᴀᴄᴇʙⲱɴ). Translation: impious (or disrespectful)
- Septuagint manuscript 664: Sabbaôn (Cⲁⲩⲩⲗoon)
- Septuagint manuscript 46: eusebôn (ⲉⲩⲟⲟⲩⲩⲧⲩn).

Translation: pious (or devout)

- Septuagint manuscript 55: Asabôn (ⲗoⲗⲩoon)
- Septuagint manuscript 637: Essebôn (Eⲟⲟⲟⲩoon)
- Aleppo Codex: šbå (שבא). Translation: Sheba (or Saba)
- Leningrad Codex: sheva (שְׁבָא). Translation: Sheba (or Saba)
- Ge'ez Bible: basan (ባሳን). Translation: Bashan
- Targum to Job: zemargad (זְמַרְגַד). Translation: Zemargad (or Zambia, Zambezi)

The Sabaeans were an ancient civilization in modern Yemen between 1200 and 275 BC. The Queen of Saba who visited King Solomon was from this civilization. They made their wealth from the overland routes across the Arabian Peninsula which competed with the shipping routes through the Red Sea due to the difficulty navigating the Red Sea.

Chapter 7

[Job continued,] "Is not the life of man on Earth a test? Is his existence like that of a day worker? Like a slave that fears his master, and one who has grabbed a shadow? Like an employee waiting for his pay? Therefore have I also endured months of vanity, and nights of pain have been inflicted on me. Whenever I lie down, I say, 'When will it be the day?' and whenever I rise again, 'I say when will it be evening?' and I am full of pains from evening to morning. My body is covered with loathsome worms, and I waste away, scraping off clods of dirt from my eruption. My life is lighter than a word and has perished in vain hope. Remember then that my life is breath, and my eye will not yet again see good."

"The eye of he that sees me will not see me again. Your eyes are on me, and I am no more. I am like a cloud that has cleared from the sky, for, if a man goes down to the grave, he will not come up again, and he will certainly not return to his own house, neither will his place know him anymore. Therefore I will not hold back my mouth, I will speak while being in distress, being in anguish I will tell the bitterness of my mind."

"Am I a sea, or a serpent, that you have set a watch over me? I said that my bed should comfort me, and I would privately counsel with myself on my couch. You scare me with dreams and terrify me with visions. You will separate life from my spirit, and yet keep my bones from death. For I will not live forever, that I should patiently endure, leave from me, for my life is vain. What is man, that you have magnified him, or that you will listen to him? Will you visit him until the morning, and judge him until the time of rest? How long until you leave me alone, or let me go, and until I will swallow down my saliva? If I have sinned, what will I be able to do, you that understand the mind of men? Why have you made me your accuser, and why am I a burden to you? Why have you not forgotten my iniquity, and purged my sin? Now, I will leave to the earth, and in the morning I will be no more."

Chapter 8

Then Bildad the Shuhites asked, "How long will you say these things? How long will the breath of your mouth be full of words? Will the Lord be unjust when he judges? Will he that has made all things pervert justice? If your sons have sinned before him, he has thrown them away because of their transgression. Instead, you should be quick in praying to God and Lord Resheph.[1] If you are pure and honest, he will listen to your prayer and will restore to you your home when you were righteous. Even though your beginning should be small, your end should be indescribably great. Ask of the former generation, and search diligently among the race of our fathers: (for we are of yesterday, and know nothing. Our life on the Earth is a shadow.) Will these not teach you, and report to you, and bring out words from their heart? Does the stream flourish without water, or will the sapling grow up without moisture? When it is yet on the root, and though it has not been cut down, does not any plant wither before it has received moisture?"

"So then will be the end of all that forget the Lord and the hope of the ungodly will perish. For his house will be without inhabitants, and his tent will become a spider's web. If he should prop up his house, it will not stand, and when he has taken hold of it, it will not remain. For it is moist under the sun, and his branch will come forth out of his dung heap. He lies down on a gath-ering of stones and lives in the middle of flints. If God should destroy him, his place will deny him. Have you not seen such things, that such is the overthrow of the ungodly? Out of the Earth, another will grow. The Lord will by no means reject the harmless man, but he will not receive any gift of the ungodly. But he will fill with laughter the mouth of the sincere, and their lips with thanksgiving. But their adversaries will clothe them-selves with shame, and the home of the ungodly will perish."

Chapter 8 Notes

1 Codex Vaticanus: cyrion pantocratora deomenos (ΚΥΡΙΟΝ ΠΑΝΤΟΚΡΑΤΟΡΑ ΔΕΟΜΕΝΟC). Translation: Lord Omnipotent to blind

- Aleppo Codex: ål-ål ûål-šdy (אל-אל ואל-שדי). Translation: god El and god Shaddai (or demonic, powerful, field, breast)
- Leningrad Codex: el-el ve'el-shaddai (אֶל־אֵל וְאֶל־שַׁדַּי). Translation: god El and god Shaddai (or demonic, powerful, field, breast)
- Targum to Job: qŏdām ĕlāhā ûlewat šaday teṣalê (קֳדָם אֱלָהָא וּלְוָת שַׁדַּי תְּצַלֵּי). Translation: neal before God and from Shaddai be saved

The Greek text includes the word "deomenos," meaning "to blind," which doesn't fit the rest of the sentence, and is generally ignored in translations. This may be a scribal error of daemonos (δαίμονος), meaning "demonic" or "godlike," suggesting the original Greek translation was similar to the Hebrew. This translation follows the Masoretic interpretation, where God and Resheph are separate gods.

Chapter 9

Then Job replied, "I know of in truth that it is like this. How will a mortal man be justified before the Lord? If he would enter into judgment with him, God would not listen to him, that he could even answer one charge in a thousand. He is wise in mind, and mighty, and great. Who has hardened himself against him and endured? Who wears out the mountains? Men don't know. Who overturns them in anger. Who shakes under the sky from its foundations, and its pillars collapse. Who commands the sun,[1] and he does not rise? Who locks up the stars?[2] Who alone has stretched out the skies, and walks on the sea like on firm ground? Who moves the Pleiades, Orion, Ursa Minor,[3] and the decans of the south?[4] Who does great and unsearchable things, glorious also and excellent things, innumerable?"

If ever he should go beyond me, I will not see him. If he should pass by me, I would not know it. If he left away, who would turn him back? Who will say to him, 'What have you done?' He has turned back anger, underneath his curves is Cetus in the lower sky.[5] If only he would hear me, or judge my case. I am righteous, but he will not listen to me! I beg his judgment. If I call and he does not listen, I can't believe that he has heard my voice. Let him not destroy me with a dark storm! He has made by many illnesses without cause, yet he allows me not to take a breath, but he has filled me with bitterness."

"Indeed he is strong and powerful, and who can resist his judgment? Though I should seem righteous, my mouth will be profane, and though I should seem blameless, I will be proved perverse. For even if I have sinned, I don't know it in my mind,[6] yet my life is taken away. Therefore I said, 'Anger kills the great and mighty man, for the worthless die. Yet the righteous are laughed at and insulted, for they are delivered into the hands of the unrighteous man.' He blindfolds the faces of the judges of the earth, and if it is not he, then who is it?"

"My life is swifter than a messenger, and my days have fled away and they did not know it. Again, is there a trace of a path left by a ship? Or is there one left by the flying eagle as it hunts its prey? If I should say, 'I will forget to speak,' I will bow down my face and groan. I quake in all my limbs, for I know that you will not leave me alone as innocent. But since I am ungodly, why have I not died? For if I should clean myself with snow, and purge myself with pure hands, you had thoroughly plunged me in filth, and my clothes have abhorred me. You are not a man like me, who I could debate with, that we might come together in agreement. If only our mediator was present, and a judge who should hear the cause between both. Let him remove his wand from me, and don't let his fear terrify me, so will I not be afraid, but I will speak, for I am not conscious of guilt."

Chapter 9 Notes

1 Codex Vaticanus: êliô (ΗΛΙѾ). Translation: Helios

• Aleppo Codex: ḥrs (חרס). Translation: clay (or pottery)

• Leningrad Codex: ḥeres (חֶרֶס). Translation: clay (or pottery)

• Targum to Job: šimša (שִׁמְשָׁא). Translation: sun

Based on the context, the word Heres is assumed to be a name of the sun. It is only used this way in Job, Joshua, and Judges, and in each case, the interpretation of the word is based on its context. It is not related to any known Semitic words meaning "sun," and may be derived from the Egyptian word ḥrt (𓏲𓊖), which translates as approximately "heaven." Ḥrt, generally anglicized as Heret, was the abode of the gods of the sky which surrounded the sun. It rose and set each day with the sun. If this is the source of the word, it suggests the text of Job was translated back into Canaanite from an Egyptian translation sometime in the late Bronze Age, as this term shifted meanings by the early Iron Age.

2 Codex Vaticanus: astrôn (ΑϹΤΡѠΝ). Translation: stars

• Aleppo Codex: kŭkbym (כוכבים). Translation: stars

• Leningrad Codex: kochavim (כּוֹכָבִים). Translation: stars

• Targum to Job: kôkebayā (כּוֹכְבַיָּא). Translation: stars

3 Codex Vaticanus: Pliada cae Hesperon cae Arctouron (ΠΛΕΙΑΔΑ ΚΑΙ ΕϹΠΕΡΟΝ ΚΑΙ ΑΡΚΤΟΥΡΟΝ). Translation: Pleiades and Hesperus and Arcturus

• Septuagint manuscript 261: Pliada cae Hesperon cae Arctouron (πλόιαγ̣ʌ̣ʌ̣ ʟ̣ʌ̣ι ϭϭπόʃ̣ʃ̣ον ʟ̣ʌ̣ι ἀʃ̣ʟ̣τουʃ̣ʌ̣). Translation: Pleiades and Hesperus and Arcturus

• Aleppo Codex: ôš ksyl ůkymh (עש כסיל וכימה). Translation: Wagon (or Ursa Minor) Fool (Orion) and Heap (or Pleiades)

• Leningrad Codex: ash kesil vechimah (עָשׁ כְּסִיל וְכִימָה). Translation: Wagon (or Ursa Minor) Fool (or Orion) and Heap (or Pleiades)

• Targum to Job: ôāš niplā wekîmā (עָשׁ נִפְלָא וְכִימָא). Translation: Wagon (or Ursa Minor) Npylyå (or Orion) and Heap (or Pleiades)

The Greek and Hebrew versions of this verse are somewhat different. Both mention the Pleiades star cluster, however, the Greek treats it as part of the four cardinal directions, also with the evening star to the west, Arcturus to the north, and the decans of the south. The Pleiades star cluster is a group of stars in the constellation of Taurus. They are easily seen in the Northern Hemisphere, as well as at equatorial latitudes, and have historically been widely used to navigate by. The Greek name is believed to derive from the word meaning 'sail' (πλέω).

The Hebrew version includes what is generally accepted as being Ursa Minor, in the form of the Wagon from Babylonian astronomy. The Greeks used the bright northern star Arcturus as a navigation point, the same as the Babylonians had used the stars of the Wagon. As such, the Greeks used the term Arcturus similar to the way a modern translator might use the name Polaris for any ancient reference to a north star, regardless of whether it was the star now called Polaris. It is recorded that in Classical literature the Greeks did sometimes translate the Wagon as Arcturus, and therefore the Greek and Hebrew texts do seem to be related, but with the Greek having loosely translated Ursa Minor (Μικρά Άρκτος) as Arcturus (Αρκτούρος).

As the Greek translation treats the Pleiades star cluster as the morning star, this would date the text to the Middle Bronze Age, approximately 2300 BC, when the Babylonian star catalogs record the Pleiades, which they called the 'stars of stars' (✸✷✸✷), were the morning stars at the vernal equinox. By the time the Greeks translated Job, it had been around 2000 years since the Pleiades were the morning stars, and therefore, they had no reason to refer to the Pleiades as the morning stars unless that was in the text they translated.

The Greek translation then refers to Hesperus, the Greek name for the planet Venus at sunset, however, the Canaanites are not recorded using a term like this, instead referring to Shalim, the god of dusk, suggesting there was a star or constellation in the text, which the Greeks interpreted as a star at dusk, and translated as Hesperus. The Hebrew version of the verse refers to Orion, in the form of Kesil, a derogatory term for Orion with translates as 'fool.' This is not the original Canaanite name for Orion, but a Late-Persian Era Hebrew name for the constellation, based on the idea that whoever worshiped it as God was a fool. The older Aramaic name of the asterism and constellation was Npylå ($\mathcal{NL}^{\wedge}\mathcal{N}$), where the Nephilim (Orionids) fell each October. The Orionids are a meteor shower that happens each year, between October 2 and November 7, as the Earth passes through the debris left by Halley's Comet. Peaks of 70 meteors a minute have been recorded, and these meteors fall from the region of the sky where Orion's upstretched arm is located.

This was the same asterism that the Old Kingdom Era Egyptians called Sah, whom they believed was the 'father of the gods (stars),' because he created new stars (gods) each October. It is worth noting that when the Pleiades were the morning stars at the vernal equinox, Orion was the evening stars that same day of the year, supporting the name Npylå as having originally been in the text the Greeks and Hebrews translated. As the name was no longer used by the time the Greeks translated the Book of Job, they would have substituted the term "evening star," which happened to be Hesperus, while the Hebrew translators clearly knew which constellation was being referred to, and translated it as "fool."

As Orion was the evening stars when the Pleiades were the morning stars, circa 2300 BC, the name Orion is imported from the Masoretic version of Job. Additionally, as the Greeks translated the Wagon as Arcturus instead of Ursa Minor, the correct modern constellation name is used in this translation.

4 Codex Vaticanus: tamia notou (ΤΑΜΙΑΝΟΤΟΥ).
Translation: housekeeper of the south
• Septuagint manuscript 55: tamian notou (τᾱμιᾱν ν⅌του).
Translation: steward of the south

- Septuagint manuscript 543: tamian notou (ⲧⲁⲙⲓⲁⲛ ⲛ̄ⲧⲟⲩ).

Translation: steward of the south

- Septuagint manuscript 620: nêmia notou (ⲛ̄ⲗⲩⲙⲓⲁ ⲛ̄ⲧⲟⲩ).

Translation: "nemia" of the south

- Septuagint manuscript 637: tamiia notou (ⲧⲁⲙⲫⲓⲁ ⲛ̄ⲧⲟⲩ).

Translation: vaults (or treasuries, stewardship) of the south

- Aleppo Codex: ḥdry tmn (חדרי תמן). Translation: rooms (or curtains) of the south

- Leningrad Codex: chadrei teman (חַדְרֵי תֵּמָן). Translation: rooms (or curtains) of the south

- Targum to Job: idrônê šitrê mazlayā bisṭar dārômā (אִדְרוֹנֵי שִׁטְרֵי מַזְלָיָא בְּסְטַר דָרוֹמָא). Translation: Adroni assigned star (or constellation) near the south

The vaults of rooms of the south are a reference to the Egyptian system of decans, known collectively as the båktů, or singularly as båkt (𓅭𓏤𓆑). They were 36 small constellations that were used to tell time at night. The decans were used since at least the Egyptian Old Kingdom Era, however, continued to be widely used throughout human history. It is believed they served as the basis for the systems of astrology that developed in India, and eventually spread as far east as Japan. The Masoretic version of Job uses an Aramaic word in this verse, one of many Aramaic words remaining in the Hebrew translation. The Greek translation includes a few variations of the alternate meaning of båkt (𓅭𓏤𓆑), which also meant female servant. This suggests that the Greek translators at the Library of Alexandria recognized that the rooms of the south were the båktu.

CHAPTER 9

The Targum of Job refers to Adroni (אָדְרוֹנִי) assigning a star or constellation in the south, which is likely a reference to the Greco-Egyptian astronomer Andronicus of Cyrrhus (Ἀνδρόνικος Κυρρήστης), who was active circa 100 BC. Andronicus was active at the Museum in Alexandria during the 1st century BC and would have known what the båktů were, however, it is unclear if he left any commentary on the Book of Job. It is more likely that a scholar studying Job made a commentary based on something Andronicus wrote about the båktů.

5 Codex Vaticanus: yp autou ecamphthêsan cêtê ta hyp ouranon (ΥΠ ΑΥΤΟΥ ΕΚΑΜΦΘΗCΑΝ ΚΗΤΗ ΤΑ ΥΠ ΟΥΡΑΝΟΝ). Translation: underneath (or under, beneath, subordinate, lower) his curves (or bends, turns) Cetus the lower (or underneath, under, beneath, subordinate) sky

• Codex Alexandrinus: hyp' autou ecamphthê cêtê ta hyp' ouranon (ΥΠ ΑΥΤΟΥ ΕΚΑΜΦΘΗ ΚΗΤΗ ΤΑ ΥΠ ΟΥΡΑΝΟΝ). Translation: underneath (or under, beneath, subordinate, lower) he fastened (or attached) Cetus the lower (or underneath, under, beneath, subordinate) sky

• Septuagint manuscript 296: ap' autou ecamphthê cêtê ta hyp' ouranon (ἀπ' ἀυτου ϭιἀμϕθὶι ιωρτὶι τἀ υπ' ουϼἀѵ8ѵ).

Translation: from he fastened (or attached) Cetus the lower (or underneath, under, beneath, subordinate) sky

• Aleppo Codex: thtů šhhů ôzry rhb (תחתו שחחו עזרי רהב).

Translation: under crouch (or stoop) helpers (or assistants) Rahab (or pride, arrogance)

• Leningrad Codex: tachatov [tachtav] shachachu ozerei rahav (תַּחַתוֹ [תַּחְתָּיו] שָׁחֲחוּ עֹזְרֵי רָהַב). Translation: under (or bottom, butt) [under (or bottom, butt)] crouch (or stoop) helpers (or assistants) rahab (or pride, arrogance)

• Targum to Job: teḥôtôy šāyeḥān rašîayā yitberûn gêwetānayā dimsayîn besûgeā (תְּחוֹתוֹי שָׁיְחָן רַשִׁיעַיָא יִתְבְּרוּן גֵּיוְתָנַיָא דְמְסִיְעִין בְּסוּגְעָא). Translation: underneath (or beneath) speaker unauthorized (or impious) sit joyfully teaching the auxiliaries frequently

Both the Greek and Hebrew translations appear to be about the constellation Cetus / Leviathan, called 'pride' in the Hebrew translation as Leviathan / Lotan / Yam had tried to usurp the throne of the Bull El in the Ba'al Cycle. The constellation Cetus / Leviathan is low in the sky, beneath the curve of the ecliptic, which is what the Greek translation is referring to. The Hebrew translation appears to be stating that the former worshipers of Leviathan / Rahab are now worshiping God / El, which is a Hellenic or Hasmonean Era theological reinterpretation of the text, as the Hebrew translator did not want to suggest that Leviathan / Rahab was himself a god that the anger of God had been one been against, but rather that the anger had been against the followers of that god.

6 Codex Vaticanus: psychê (ⲯⲨⲬⲎ). Translation: mind (or personality, psyche, soul)

• Aleppo Codex: npšy (נפשׁי). Translation: mind (or psyche, life)

CHAPTER 9

- Leningrad Codex: nafshi (נַפְשִׁי). Translation: mind (or psyche, life)
- Targum to Job: teḥôtôy napšî (נַפְשִׁי). Translation: mind (or psyche, life)

Chapter 10

[Job continued,] "I am tired in my mind, and I will pour my words with moaning upon him. I will speak directly about the bitterness of my mind. I will say to the Lord, 'Do not teach me to be impious! Why have you thus judged me? Does it sit well with you that I am judged unrighteous? You have disowned the work of your hands, and attended to the counsel of the ungodly! Or do you see as a mortal sees? Will you see as a man sees? Is your life human, and your years the years of a man, that you have inquired into my iniquity and searched out my sins? You know that I have not committed iniquity! But who is it that can deliver out of your hands? Your hands have formed me and made me, and afterward, you changed your mind and injured me. Remember that you have molded me like clay, yet you throw me back to dirt. Have you not poured me out like milk, and curdled me like cheese? Did you clothe me with skin and flesh, and frame me with bones and sinews? Did you bestow on me life and mercy, and your oversight preserved my spirit? Having these things in yourself, I know that you can do all things, for nothing is impossible with you."

"If I should sin, you saw me, and you have not cleared me from iniquity. If I am ungodly, woe for me! If I am righteous, I can't lift myself as I am full of dishonor. I am hunted like a lion for slaughter, for you have changed and are destroying me, torturing me, and have dealt with me in great anger, and you have brought trials on me! Why then did you bring me out of the womb? Why did I not die, and no eye see me, and I become as if I had not been? Why was I not carried from the womb to the grave? Is not the time of my life short? Allow me to rest a little, before I go from where I will not return, to a land of darkness and gloominess, to a land of perpetual darkness, where there is no light, and where no one can see the life of living."[1]

Chapter 10 Notes

1 This description of the 'land of perpetual darkness' is remarkably similar to the descriptions of the underworld found in Sumerian and Akkadian literature from the 3rd millennium BC, and Babylonian literature from the 2nd millennium BC. The Sumerian texts used several names including Arali, Irkalla, Kukku, Ekur, Kigal, and Ganzir, while the latter Akkadian and Babylonian texts generally used the term Erṣetu, the Semitic forerunner of the modern Hebrew Eretz (אֶרֶץ) which means country, land, ground, or soil, depending on context.

Chapter 11

Then Zophar the Minaean replied, "He who says much should be heard on the other side, or does the fluent speaker think himself to be righteous? Blessed is the short-lived offspring of a woman. Do not be a speaker of many words, but allow another to answer you. Don't say, 'I am pure in my works, and blameless before him.' If only the Lord would speak to you, and open his lips to you! Then will he tell you the power of wisdom, as it is twice of that which is within you. Then you would know that a just repayment of your sins has come upon you from the Lord. Will you even follow the magnificent words of the Lord, or influence Resheph? The sky[1] is high, and what will you do? There are deeper things than Sheol,[2] what do you know? Longer than the measure of the earth, or the width of the sea. If he should overthrow all things, who will say to him, 'What have you done?' For he knows the works of transgressors, and when he sees wickedness, he will not overlook it. But man vainly buoys himself up with words, and a mortal born of a woman is like a donkey in the desert."

"If you have made your heart pure, lift your hands towards him. If there is any iniquity in your hands, put it far from you, and don't let unrighteousness stay in your home. And so will your countenance shine again, as pure water, and you will dive uncleanness from yourself, and will not fear. You will forget the trouble like a wave that has passed by, and you will not be scared. Your prayer is like the morning star, and life will rise to you from noonday. You will be confident, because you have hope, and peace will dawn for you from out of anxiety and care. For you will be at ease, and there will be no one to fight against you. Many will come and beg to you, but safety will fail them, for their hope is destruction, and the eyes of the ungodly will waste away."

Chapter 11 Notes

1 Codex Vaticanus: ouranos (ΟΥΡΑΝΟϹ). Translation: vaulted sky (or Uranus, roof)

• Septuagint manuscript 46: ouranos gê de bathia (ΟΥΡΑΝΟϹΓΗΔΕΒΑΘΕΙΑ). Translation: vaulted sky land in the heights

• Aleppo Codex: šmym (שמים). Translation: skies (or Shamayim)

• Leningrad Codex: šāmayim (שָׁמַיִם). Translation: skies (or Shamayim)

• Targum to Job: šemayā (שְׁמַיָּא). Translation: sky (or heaven)

The sky (Shamayim / Uranus) is depicted as the same type of primordial deity in the Septuagint as it was in the Greek myths and called on to witness blessings and curses, implying consciousness. The name Uranus (Οὐρανός) was derived from the Amorite term ùruanna (𒀭𒂍𒊺𒉽𒆠), meaning 'roof sky stone,' which was also the Greek description of Uranus, as the ceiling above the flat Earth. This term appears to have been absorbed into Greek as the name Uranus during the Greek Dark Age, after the collapse of the Mycenaean civilization, as the name has not been documented in Linear-B, the script of the Mycenaeans.

The term in the Masoretic Text, šāmayim is the Hebrew word for "skies," however, is also the name of the ancient Semitic sky god, spelled as Šamuû (𒀭𒈹) in Akkadian Cuneiform, Šmyn (𐎌𐎎𐎐) in Ugaritic, Šmm (𐤔𐤌𐤌) in Canaanite, Smyn (𐩦𐩣𐩬) in Sabaean, and Šmyn (ܫܡܝܢ) in Aramaic.

2 Codex Vaticanus: adou (ⲀⲆⲞⲨ). Translation: Hades
• Aleppo Codex: šåûl (שָׁאוּל). Translation: netherworld (or Saul)
• Leningrad Codex: she'ol (שְׁאוֹל). Translation: netherworld (or grave)
• Targum to Job: šêôl (שְׁיוֹל). Translation: netherworld (or grave)

The specific spelling of Hades in the Septuagint makes it clear that it is a reference to the Greek underworld and not the god Hades. Based on the earlier description of the 'land of perpetual darkness' in the previous chapter, this reference to Hades cannot be interpreted as the Greek fiery underworld, but more like the Erṣetu of the Babylonians. The traditional Canaanite land of the dead was Mirey (𒆳𒈾𒄀), the land ruled by Mot the god of the dead, who was later seen by the ancient Hebrews as the angel of death, according to the books of Habakkuk, Hosea, and Jeremiah.

Chapter 12

Job replied, "So then you alone are men, and wisdom will die with you? Yet I also have a heart like you, and a righteous and blameless man has become a subject for mockery. It had been ordained that he should fall under others at the appointed time and that his houses should be spoiled by criminals. However, don't let anyone trust that being evil, he will be held guiltless, even as many as have provoked the Lord, as if there were indeed to be no inquiry made of them. But ask now the animals, if they will speak to you, and the birds of the air, if they will speak to you. Ask the Earth if it will speak to you and if the fish of the sea will explain to you. Who then has not known in all these things, that the hand of the Lord has made them?"

"The life of all living things is in his hand and the breath of every man. The ear hears words, and the tongue tastes food. After a length of time comes wisdom, and in a long life comes knowledge. With him are wisdom and power, with him counsel and understanding. If he knocks over, who will rebuild? If he should lock up against man, who will open? If he should withhold the water, he will dry the earth, and if he should let it loose, he floods and destroys it. With him are strength and power, and he has knowledge and understanding. He leads counselors away captive, and maddens the judges of the earth."

CHAPTER 12

"He seats kings on thrones and clothes their bodies with a girdle. He sends away priests into captivity and overthrows the mighty ones of the earth. He changes the lips of the trusty, and he knows the understanding of the elders. He pours dishonor on princes, and heals the lowly, revealing deep things out of the darkness. He has brought into light the shadow of death, causing the nations to wander and destroying them, overthrowing the nations, and leading them away, confusing the minds of the princes of the Earth. He causes them to wander along a path they have not known, saying, "Let them grope in darkness, and let there be no light, and let them wander like a drunken man."

Chapter 13

[Job continued,] "Look, my eyes have seen these things, and my ears have heard them. I know all you to know, and I have no less understanding than you. Nevertheless, I will speak to the Lord, and I will reason before him if he will permit it. But you are all bad physicians and healers of diseases. If you were silent, it would show more wisdom in the end. Hear the reasoning from my mouth, and listen to the judgment of my lips. Do you not speak before the Lord, and tell lies before him? Or will you withdraw? No, do you judge? It would be well if he would thoroughly search you, for even though doing all things in your power you should attach yourselves to him, and he would not reprove you any less. Moreover, if you should secretly marvel at faces, would not his fear sweep you away, and terror of him fall on you? Your glorying will prove in the end to you like ashes, and your body like a body of clay."

"Be silent, that I may speak, and end my anger. While I may take my flesh in my teeth, and put my life in my hand, if I am manipulated by an abuser, as he has done, still I will speak and plead before him. This will return to me as salvation, for fraud will have no entrance before him. Hear, hear my words, for I will declare in your hearing. Look, I am near my judgment. I know that I will eventually appear just. For who is he that will plead with me, that I should now be silent, and expire? Grant me two things, and I will not hide from your face. With-hold your hand from me, and don't let you be afraid of terrifying me. When you call, I will listen to you. You will speak and I will give you an answer. How many are my sins and my transgressions? Tell me what they are. Why hide yourself from me, and treat me as your enemy? Are you scared of me, like a leaf shaken by the wind? Will you set yourself against me like against grass carried on the breeze? You have written evil things against me, and you have surrounded me with the sins of my youth. You have placed my foot in the stocks, and you have watched all my works, and have penetrated my heels. I am as that which grows old like a bottle, or like a moth-eaten garment."

Chapter 14

[Job continued,] "A mortal born of a woman is short-lived and full of anger. He falls like a flower that has bloomed, and he departs like a shadow, and can't continue. Have you not taken account even of him, and caused him to enter into judgment before you? Who will be pure from uncleanness? Not even one! If even his life should be only one day on the earth, and his months are counted by him, you have appointed him for a time, and he will by no means exceed it. Leave from him, that he may be quiet, and take pleasure in his life, though as an employee. For there is hope for a tree, even if it should be cut down, that it will blossom again, and its branch will not fail. Though its root should grow old in the earth, and its stem dies in the rock, it will blossom from the scent of water, and will produce a crop, like one newly planted."

"But a man that has died, he is completely gone, and when a mortal has fallen, he is no more. For the sea dries after a length of time, and a river fails and is dried up. Man that has laid down in death will certainly not rise again until the sky is dissolved, and they will not awake from their sleep. If only you had kept me in the grave and had hidden me until your anger should cease, and you should set me a time in which you would remember me! For if a man should die, will he live again, having finished the days of his life? Will I wait until I exist again? Then will you call, and I will listen to you but do not you reject the work of your hands. You have counted my devices, and not one of my sins will escape you. You have sealed up my transgressions in a bag, and marked if I have been guilty of any transgression without knowing. A falling mountain will completely be destroyed, and a rock will be worn out of its place. The waters wear the stones, and waters falling headlong overflow a heap of the earth, and you destroy the hope of man. You drive him to an end, and he is gone. You set your face against him and send him away, and though his children are multiplied, he does not know it, and if they are few, he is not aware. His flesh is in pain, and his mind mourns."

Chapter 15

Then Eliphaz the Temanite answered, "Will a wise man give a few breaths of wisdom and answer? Does he fill up the pain of his belly, reasoning with improper sayings, and with words in which there is no profit? Have not you thrown off fear, and accomplished such words before the Lord? You are guilty by the words of your mouth, and neither have you discerned the words of the Lord. Let your own mouth, and not mine, reprove you and your lips will testify against you. What? Are you the first man that was born? Were you established before the hills? Have you heard the commands of the Lord? Has God used you as his counselor? Has wisdom only come to you? For what do you know, that we don't know? What do you understand, which we do not also know?"

"Truly, among us are both the old and very aged man, more advanced in days than your father. You have been scourged for but few of your sins. You have spoken haughtily and extravagantly. What has your heart dared? What have your eyes looked at, that you have vented your rage before the Lord, and delivered such words from your mouth? For who, being a mortal, is blameless? Who is born from a woman, is just when he does not trust his ordained?[1] Is the sky not seen as pure by him? Alas then, abominable and unclean is man, drinking unrighteousness like a draft. I will tell you, listen to me, and I will tell you now what I have seen, the things wise men say, and their fathers have not hidden. To them alone, the earth was given, and no alien came on them. All the life of the ungodly is spent in care, and the years granted to the oppressor are counted. His terror is in his ears. Just when he seems to be at peace, his overthrow will come. Let him not trust that he will return from darkness, for he has been already made over to the power of the sword."

"He has been appointed to be food for vultures, and he knows within himself that he is doomed to be a carcass, and a dark day will carry him away with an iron hand. Distress and anguish will come over him, and he will fall as a captain in the first rank. He has lifted his hands against the Lord, and he has hardened his neck against Resheph. He has run against him with insolence, on the thickness of the back of his shield. For he has covered his face with his fat and made layers of fat on his thighs. Let him remain in desolate cities, and enter into houses without inhabitants, and what they have prepared, others will carry away. He will neither grow rich at all, nor will his property remain, and he will not cast a shadow on the earth. He will not in any way escape the darkness. Let the wind blast his blossom, and let his flower fall off. Let him not think that he will endure, for his end will be vanity. His harvest will perish before the time, and his branch will not flourish. Let him be gathered as the unripe grape before the time, and let him fall as the blossom of the olive. For death is the witness of an ungodly man, and fire will burn the houses of them that receive gifts. He will conceive sorrows, and his end will be vanity, and his belly will carry deceit."

Chapter 15 Notes

1 Codex Vaticanus: hagiôn (ᎪᎾⲓⲰN). Translation: sacred ones (or saints)
- Aleppo Codex: bqdšů (בקדשו). Translation: his ordained (or sanctified)
- Leningrad Codex: vkdshv [bikdoshav] (בְקְדֹשָׁיו |בִקְדֹשׁו). Translation: his ordained [his saints]
- Targum to Job: beqadîšê (בְקַדִּישֵׁי). Translation: his saints

In the Late Bronze Age, Qadesh was the title of the Canaanite goddess Asherah and the Egyptian goddess Hathor, both of which represented the sky. The worship of Qadesh seems to have been focused in the city of Kadesh, in modern Syria. She was also worshiped in King Solomon's Temple, along with Baal until the ban on all gods other than Yahweh under King Josiah. This verse seems to be referring to the stars as 'ordained ones,' suggesting the text was used by the worshipers of Asherah.

Chapter 16

Job replied, "I have heard many similar things. You are all poor comforters. Why? Is there any reason in vain words? What will stop you from answering? I also will speak as you do, as if indeed your mind were in my mind's place, and then I would insult you with words, and I would shake my head at you. If there were strength in my mouth, I would not spare the movement of my lips. For if I should speak, I will not feel the pain of my wound, and if I should be silent, how will I be wounded the less? But now he has made me weary and a worn-out fool, and you have laid hold of me. My lies have become a testimony, and have risen up against me, and have confronted me to my face. In his anger, he has thrown me down, and he has gnashed his teeth on me, and the weapons of his robbers have fallen on me."

"He has attacked me with the keen glances of his eyes with his sharp spear, he has struck me down on my knees, and they have run against me with one accord. The Lord has delivered me into the hands of unrighteous men and thrown me on the ungodly. When I was at peace, he distracted me, and he took me by the hair of the head and plucked it out, and he set me up as a mark. They surrounded me with spears, aiming at my veins, without sparing me they poured out my guts on the ground. They overthrew me with fall after fall, and they ran against me in their strength. They sewed sackcloth on my skin, and my strength has been spent on the ground. My belly has been parched with wailing, and darkness is on my eyelids."

"Yet there was no injustice in my hands, and my prayer is pure. Eretz,[1] don't cover over the blood of my flesh and let my cry have no place. Now, look, my witness is Shamayim,[2] and my advocate is up high. Let my supplication come to the Lord, and let my eye cry before him. If only a man might plead before the Lord, even as the son of man with his neighbor! But my years are counted and their end comes, and I will go by the way by which I will not return."

Chapter 16 Notes

1 Codex Vaticanus: Gê (ΓΗ). Translation: Ge (or land, earth, country, soil)

• Aleppo Codex: årṣ (אֶרֶץ). Translation: Eretz (or land, earth, country, soil)

• Leningrad Codex: eretz (אֶרֶץ). Translation: Eretz (or land, earth, country, soil)

• Targum to Job: arôã (אַרְעָא). Translation: land (or dirt, country)

The Earth (Ge, Eretz) is depicted as the same type of primordial deity in the Septuagint as it was in the Greek myths and is called on to witness blessings and curses, implying consciousness. This view continues in Judahite texts until at least the 2nd century BC as demonstrated in the Testaments of the Patriarchs.

2 Codex Vaticanus: Ouranoes (ΟΥΡΑΝΟΙϹ). Translation: Uranus (or skies)

- Codex Sinaiticus: Ouranô (ΟΥΡΑΝѠ). Translation: skies
- Aleppo Codex: šmym (שמים). Translation: Shamayim (or skies, vaulted sky)
- Leningrad Codex: shamayim (שָׁמַיִם). Translation: Shamayim (or skies, vaulted sky)
- Targum to Job: šemayā (שְׁמַיָּא). Translation: sky

As the author is clearly calling on the sky god Shamayim, his name is restored from the Masoretic text.

Chapter 17

[Job continued,] "I die carried away by the wind, and I search for burial but do not obtain it. Weary I beg, 'What have I done?' Aliens have stolen my goods. Who is this? Let him join hands with me. For you have hidden their heart from wisdom, therefore you will not exalt them. He will promise mischief to his companions, but their eyes have failed for their children. You have made me an insult among the nations, and I have become contemptible to them. My eyes are dimmed through pain, and I have been grievously beset by all. Amazement has seized honest men on this, and let the just rise against the transgressor. But let the faithful hold on his way, and let him that is pure of hands take courage. How is it, do you all strengthen yourselves and come now, if I do not find honesty in you?"

"My days have passed in groaning, and my heartstrings are broken. I have turned the night into day, the light is short because of darkness. For if I remain, Sheol is my home, and my bed has been made in darkness. I have called on Mot[1] to be my father, and corruption to be my mother and sister. Where then is yet my hope? Where will I see my good? Will they go down with me to Sheol, or will we go down together to the tomb?"

Chapter 17 Notes

1 Codex Vaticanus: Thanaton (ⲐⲀⲚⲀⲦⲞⲚ). Translation: Thanatos (or death)

- Aleppo Codex: šḥt (שחת). Translation: corruption
- Leningrad Codex: shachat (שַׁחַת). Translation: corruption
- Targum to Job: šaḥtā (שְׁחָתָא). Translation: pit (or hemorrhoids, worms)

This verse reads differently in the Masoretic Text, as Job called corruption (שַׁחַת) his father, and the hills (רִמָּה) his mother and sister. As the Greek Thanatos was a translation for the Canaanite god of death Mot, and Israelite messenger of death Mot, Mot is used in this translation. While the verses are different, it is clear that the word 'corruption' was in the text that the Greeks translated. The word in the Masoretic text is šht (שחת), meaning 'hay' in Hebrew or Canaanite, and 'rust' or 'corruption' in Aramaic, supporting the Greek translation as having been made from an Aramaic text.

Chapter 18

Then Bildad the Shuhite asked, "How long will you continue? Restrain yourself, so we can also speak. Why have we been silent before you like animals? Anger has possessed you! What if you die? Will all the land under the sky become desolate? Will the mountains be overthrown from their foundations? The light of the ungodly will be quenched, and their flame will not go up. His light will be darkness in his home, and his lamp will be put out with him. Let the meanest of men spoil his goods, and let his counsel deceive him. His foot also has been caught in a snare, and let it be caught in a net. Let snares come on him, and he will strengthen those who thirst for his destruction. His snare is hidden in the earth, and that which will take him is by the path. Let pains destroy him all around, and let many enemies come about him, and trouble him with distressing hunger."

"A destruction signal has been prepared for him. Let the soles of his feet be devoured, and death will consume his beauty. Let health be completely banished from his tent, and let distress seize on him with an order from the king. It will live in his tent in his night, and his excellency will be sown with brimstone. His roots will be dried up from beneath, and his crop will fall away from above. Let his memorial perish out of the earth, and his name will be publicly thrown out. Let one drive him from light into darkness. He will not be known among his people, nor his house preserved on the earth. But strangers will live in his possessions, and the last groaned for him, and wonder seized the first. These are the houses of the unrighteous, and this is the place of those that don't know the Lord."

Chapter 19

Then Job answered, "How long will you trouble my mind, and destroy me with words? Only know that the Lord has dealt with me like this. You speak against me, and you do not feel for me but carry hard on me. Yes verily, I have erred in truth, (but the error abides with myself) in having spoken words which it was not right to speak, and my words error, and are unreasonable. But alas! You magnify yourselves against me and insult me with reproach. Know then that it is the Lord that has troubled me, and has raised his bulwark against me. Look, I laugh at reproach. I will not speak, or I will cry out, but there is no judgment. I am fenced round about, and can by no means escape, and he has set darkness before my face. He has stripped me of my glory and has taken the crown from my head. He has torn me around about, and I am gone, and he has cut off my hope like a tree. He has dreadfully handled me in anger and has counted me as an enemy. His troops also came on me with one accord, liars in wait compassed my ways. My brothers have stood apart from me, and they have recognized strangers rather than me, and my friends have become pitiless."

"My nearest of kin have not acknowledged me, and they that knew my name, have forgotten me. As for my household, and my maidservants, I was a stranger before them. I called my servant, and he did not listen, and my mouth begged him. I implored my wife and earnestly begged the sons of my concubines. But they rejected me forever, and whenever I rose, they spoke against me. They that saw me abhorred me, and the very persons whom I had loved, rose against me. My flesh is corrupt under my skin, and my bones are held in my teeth. Pity me, pity me, friends, for it is the hand of the Lord that has touched me. Therefore do you persecute me as also the Lord does, and are not satisfied with my flesh? For oh that my words were written, and that they were recorded in a book forever, with an iron pen and lead, or graven in the rocks! For I know that he is eternal who is about to deliver me and to raise up on the earth my skin that endures these allowing, and for these things have been accomplished to me of the Lord, which I am conscious of in myself, which my eye has seen, and not another, but all have been fulfilled to me in my bosom. But if you will also say, "What will we say before him, and so find the root of the matter in him? Do you also beware of deceit, for anger will come on transgressors, and then will they know where their substance is?"

Chapter 20

Then Zophar the Minaean asked, "I don't suppose that you will answer this, or that you understand more than I do. I will hear my shameful reproach, and the spirit of my understanding answers me. Have you not known these things of old, from the time that man was set on the earth? But the mirth of the ungodly is a signal of downfall, and the joy of transgressors is destruction, and although his gifts should go up to the sky, his sacrifice reaches the clouds. For when he will seem to be now established, then he will completely perish, and they that knew him will say, 'Where is he?' Like a dream that has fled away, he will not be found, and he has fled like a vision of the night. The eye has looked on him, but will not see him again, and his place will no longer perceive him."

"Let his inferiors destroy his children, and let his hands kindle the fire of sorrow. His bones have been filled with the vigor of his youth, and it will lie down with him in the dust. Though evil is sweet in his mouth, though he will hide it under his tongue, and though he will not spare it, and will not leave it, but will keep it among his throat, yet he will not at all be able to help himself, with the guts of an asp is in his belly. His wealth unjustly collected will be vomited up, and a messenger of anger will drag him out of his house. Let him suck the poison of serpents, and let the serpent's tongue kill him.

Let him not see the milk of the pastures, nor the supplies of honey and butter. He has labored unprofitably and in vain, for the wealth of which he will not taste, and it is as a lean thing, unfit for food, which he can't swallow."

"He has broken down the houses of many mighty men, and he has plundered a home, though he built it not. There is no security to his possessions, and he will not be saved by his desire. Nothing is remaining of his provisions, and therefore his goods will not flourish. But when he will seem to be just satisfied, he will be straightened, and all distress will come on him. If by any means he would fill his belly, let God send on him the fury of anger, and let him bring a torrent of pains on him. He will by no means escape from the power of the sword, and let the bronze bow wound him. Let the arrow pierce through his body, and let the stars be against his living-place, and let terrors come on him. Let all darkness wait for him, a fire that burns not out will consume him, and let a stranger plague his house. Let the sky reveal his iniquities, and the Earth rise up against him. Let destruction bring his house to an end, and let a day of anger come on him. This is the portion of an ungodly man from the Lord, and the possession of his goods appointed him by the all-seeing God."

Chapter 21

Job answered, "Hear my words, that I may not have this consolation from you. Raise me up, and I will speak, and then you will not laugh and insult me. What is my reproof from man? Why should I not be angry? Look at me, and wonder, laying your hand on your cheek. For even when I remember, I am alarmed, and pains seize my flesh. Why do the ungodly live, and grow old even in wealth? Their seed is according to their desire, and their children are in their sight. Their houses are prosperous, neither have they any cause for fear, neither is there a punishment from the Lord on them. Their cow does not abandon her calf, and their animal with young is safe and does not miscarry. They remain as an unfailing flock, and their children play before them, taking up the lute and harp, and they rejoice at the voice of a song. They spend their days in wealth and fall asleep in the rest of the grave. Yet such a man says to the Lord, 'Leave from me, and I don't desire to know your ways. What is Resheph, that we should serve him? What profit is there that we should approach him? For their good things were in their hands, but he regards not the works of the ungodly. Nevertheless, the lamp of the ungodly also will be put out, and destruction will come on them, and struggles of vengeance will seize them. They will be as chaff before the wind, or as dust which the storm has taken up. Let his substance fail to supply his children. God will recompense him, and he will know it. Let his eyes see his own destruction, and let him not be saved by the Lord. For his desire to be in his house with him, and the number of his months has been suddenly cut off. Is it not the Lord who teaches understanding and knowledge? Does not he judge murderers? One will die in his perfect strength, and wholly at ease and prosperous, and his inwards are full of fat, and his marrow is diffused throughout him. Another dies in bitterness of mind, not eating anything good. They lie down in the earth together, and corruption covers them.'"

"So I know you that you presumptuously attack me, and you say, 'Where is the house of the prince? Where is the covering of the tabernacles of the ungodly?' Ask those that go by the way, and do not disown their tokens. For the wicked rushes to the day of destruction, and they will be led away for the day of his vengeance. Who will tell him his way to his face, whereas he has done it? Who will repay him? He has been led away to the tombs, and he has watched over the heaps. The stones of the valley have been sweet to him, and every man will leave after him, and there are innumerable ones before him. How then do you comfort me in vain? Whereas I have no rest from your molestation."

Chapter 22

Then Eliphaz the Temanite replied, "Is it not the Lord that teaches understanding and knowledge? What matters to the Lord if you were blameless in your works? Is it profitable that you should perfect your way? Will you maintain and plead your own cause? Will he enter into judgment with you? Is not your wickedness abundant, and your sins innumerable? You have taken security of your brothers for nothing, and have taken away the clothing of the naked. Neither have you given water to the thirsty to drink, but have taken away the morsel of the hungry. You have accepted the persons of some, and you have established those that were already settled on the earth. But you have sent widows away empty, and have afflicted orphans."

"Therefore snares have captured you, and disastrous war has troubled you. The light has proved darkness to you, and water has covered you when you lay down. Does not he that dwells in the high places see it? Has he not brought down the proud? You have said, "What does Resheph know? Does he judge in the dark? A cloud is his hiding place, and he will not be seen, and he passes through the circle of the sky. Won't you mark the old path, which righteous men have trodden? Who was seized before their time, their foundations are as an overflowing stream. Who says, 'What will the Lord do to us?' or 'What will Resheph bring on us?' Yet he filled their houses with good things, but the counsel for the wicked is far from him. The righteous have seen it and laughed, and the blameless one has derided them. Verily their substance has been completely destroyed, and the fire will devour what is left of their property. Be firm, I beg you, if you can endure, and then your fruit will prosper. Receive a declaration from his mouth, and lay up his words in your heart. If you will turn and humiliate yourself before the Lord, you have thus removed unrighteousness far from your home."

"You will lay up for yourself treasure in a heap on the rock, and Sauvira[1] will be as the rock of the torrent. So Resheph will be your helper from enemies, and he will bring you forth pure as silver that has been tried by fire. Will you have boldness before the Lord, looking up cheerfully to the sky? He will hear you when you pray to him, and he will grant you the power to pay your vows. He will establish to you again a home of righteousness and there will be light on your paths. Because you have humiliated yourself, and you will say, 'Man has behaved proudly, but he will save him that is of lowly eyes.' He will deliver the innocent, and do you save yourself by your pure hands."

Chapter 22 Notes

1 Codex Vaticanus: Ôphir (ⲱϥⲓⲣ)

• Septuagint manuscript 55: Sôphêr (ⲥⲱϥⲗⲣ)

• Septuagint manuscript 249: Sophir (ⲥⲟϥⲟⲓⲣ)

• Septuagint manuscript 644: Soupheir (ⲥⲟⲩϥⲟⲓⲣ)

• Septuagint manuscript 795: Saphir (ⲥⲁϥⲟⲓⲣ)

• Septuagint manuscript 797: Ophir (ⲟϥⲟⲓⲣ)

• Aleppo Codex: Åûpyr (אוֹפִיר)

• Leningrad Codex: Ofir (אוֹפִיר)

• Bohairic manuscripts: Sûpheir (ⲥⲱϥⲉⲓⲣ)

• Ge'ez Bible: Sefer (ሰፈር)

• Targum to Job: âôpîr (אוֹפִיר)

Some of the manuscripts of the Septuagint's Book of Job contain a curious spelling of this name Ôphir (Ωφιρ), which is very similar to the name in the Masoretic text. In other manuscripts, and most other places in the Septuagint, it is spelled as variations of Sôphêra (Σωφηρα). As the Greeks had no idea where this was, they had no reason to alter the spelling, suggesting that the Book of Job was translated into Aramaic from southern Canaanite dialect, such as Paleo-Hebrew, as the alternate name of Sôphera is found in books originally written in Aramaic, such as the books of Kingdoms (Masoretic Samuel and Kings).

The location of this civilization has been a matter of debate for centuries. Given the list of items in the books of the Kingdoms imported from Sôphêra/Ôphir, it was likely the ancient Pakistani Kingdom of Sauvira on the Indus River.

Imported items include gold, silver, sandalwood, pearls, ivory, apes, and peacocks. Sandalwood trees are indigenous to South and Southeast Asia and have traditionally been considered sacred by the Hindus, Jainists, Buddhists, and Zoroastrians, as well as other Asian cultures. Peacocks are indigenous to South and Southeast Asia, as well as the Congo Rain-forest, however, Sandalwood trees are not found in the Congo Rain-forest. Apes were still living in South and Southeast Asia circa 1000 BC, along with most of Africa.

An alternate theory regarding the location of Sôphêra was that it was a trading port in Southern Arabia or Somalia, however, the ships of Solomon were said to take three years to travel between Edom and Sôphêra/Ôphir, which makes the location of Sauvira more likely. The Kingdom of Sauvira is listed in the ancient Late Vedic period and early Buddhist literature, as well as the Mahabharata, based around its capital of Rohri in the modern Pakistani state of Sindh. The Kingdom of Sauvira is believed to have developed in the aftermath of the decline of the Harappan Civilization and therefore is generally assumed to have not existed before 1300 BC, making it either a later addition to the Book of Job, or a name that was substituted for a land the Canaanite translators did not recognize.

This reference could have been to the ancient Harappan civilization in Pakistan and northwestern India, but there is nothing in Job to identify it other than the reference to gold. As gold was a major commodity since before 5000 BC, this does not help identify the land. Major ancient sources of gold existed in Egypt, Sudan, Spain, and India. As Kush is later mentioned in the text, it seems unlikely the reference was to Sudan, Egypt is not mentioned in the Book of Job, which suggests it was translated into Aramaic in Judah during the Nubian Dynasty of Egypt, between 747 and 656 BC, which would explain the Hebrew pronunciation of the name instead of the Aramaic pronunciation. As the name was probably a substitute for another earlier name, but that name is unknown, the name is transliterated directly in this translation.

Chapter 23

Then Job replied, "Yes, I know that pleading is out of my reach, and his hand has been made heavy on my groaning. Who would then know that I might find him, and come to an end of the matter? I would plead my own cause, and he would fill my mouth with arguments. I would know the remedies which he would speak to me, and I would perceive what he would tell me. Though he should come on me in his great strength, then he would not threaten me, for truth and reproof are from him, and he would bring forth my judgment to an end. For if I will go first, and exist no longer, still what do I know concerning the latter end? When he worked on the left hand, then I did not see it. His right hand will encompass me but I will not see it. For he knows already my way, and he has tested me like gold. I will go out according to his commandments, for I have kept his ways, and I will not turn aside from his commandments, neither will I transgress, but I have hidden his words in my bosom."

"If too he has thus judged, who is he that has contradicted, for he has both desired something and then done it. Therefore am I troubled at him, and when I was reproved, I thought of him. Therefore let me take good heed before him: I will consider, and be afraid of him. But the Lord has softened my heart, and Resheph has troubled me. I did not know that darkness would come on me, and thick darkness has covered me before my face."

Chapter 24

[Job continued,] "But why have the seasons been hidden from the Lord, while the ungodly have passed over the bound, carrying off the flock with the shepherd? They have led away, the donkey of the fatherless, and taken the widow's ox for a pledge. They have turned aside from the weak from the right way, and the meek of the earth have hidden themselves together. They have departed like asses in the field, having gone out on my account according to their own order, and his bread is sweet to his little ones. They have reaped a field that was not their own before the time, and the poor have labored in the vineyards of the ungodly without pay and without food. They have caused many naked to sleep without clothes, and they have taken away the covering of their body. They are wet with the drops of the mountains, and they have embraced the rock because they had no shelter. They have snatched the fatherless from the breast, and have afflicted the outcast. They have wrongfully caused others to sleep without clothing, and taken away the morsel of the hungry. They have unrighteously laid wait in narrow places, and have not known the righteous way. Who has thrown out the poor from the city and their own houses, and the mind of the children has groaned aloud."

"Why then has he not visited these? As they were on the Earth and took no notice, and they did not know the way of righteousness, neither have they walked in their appointed paths? Having known their works, he delivered them into darkness, and in the night one will be as a thief, and the eye of the adulterer has watched for the darkness, saying, 'Eye will not see me, and he puts a covering on his face. In the darkness, he digs through houses, and by day they conceal themselves securely, and they don't know the light. For the morning is to them all as the shadow of death, for each will be conscious of the terror of the shadow of death. He is swift on the face of the water, and let his portion be cursed on the earth, and let their plants be laid bare. Let them be withered on the earth, for they have plundered the sheaves of the fatherless. Then is his sin brought to remembrance, and he vanishes like a vapor of dew. Let what he has done be recompensed to him, and let every unrighteous one be crushed like rotten wood. For he has not treated the barren woman well and has had no pity on a weak woman. In anger, he has overthrown the helpless, and therefore when he has risen, a man will not feel secure in his own life. When he has fallen sick, let him not hope to recover, and let him perish by disease. For his exaltation has hurt many, but he has withered as mallows in the heat, or as an ear of grain falling off of itself from the stalk. But if not, who is he that says I speak falsely and will make my words of no account?"

Chapter 25

Then Bildad the Shuhite asked, "What is this preamble to fear of him? He who makes all things in the highest? Let none think that there is a respite for robbers, and on whom will there not come a snare from him? For how will a mortal be just before the Lord? Who that is born of a woman will purify himself? If he gives an order to the moon, then it shines not, and the stars are not pure before him. But alas! Man is corruption, and the son of man, a worm."

Chapter 26

Job answered, "To whom do you attach yourself? Who are you going to serve? Isn't it he who has much strength, and he who has a strong arm? To whom have you given counsel? Is it not to he who has all wisdom? Who will you follow? Is it not one who has the greatest power? To whom have you said words? Whose breath is it that has come out from you? Will Raphites[1] be delivered from under the water and their neighbors? Sheol is naked before him, and Abaddon[2] has no robe. He stretches out the north wind on nothing, and he hangs the earth on nothing, binding water in his clouds, and the cloud is not torn under it. He keeps back the face of his throne, stretching out his cloud on it. He has surrounded the face of the water by an appointed ordinance, until the end of light and darkness. The pillars of the sky are prostrate and astonished at his rebuke. He has calmed the sea with his might, and by his wisdom, the Cetus has been overthrown. The barriers of the sky fear him, and by his command, he has killed the apostate dragon.[3] Look, these are parts of his way, and we will listen to him at the least intimation of his word? Who knows when he will employ the power of his thunder?"[4]

Chapter 26 Notes

1 Codex Vaticanus: Gigantes (ΓΙΓΑΝΤΕϹ). Translation: Gigantes

• Codex Sinaiticus: gitones (ΓΕΙΤΟΝΕϹ). Translation: neighbors

• Aleppo Codex: Rpåym (רפאים). Generally transliterated as Raphites

• Leningrad Codex: Refa'im (רְפָאִים). Generally transliterated as Raphites.

• Targum to Job: gibbārayā (גִבָּרִיָא). Translation: man

The Greek Gigantes were an ancient race of men or demigods that fought the gods and lost. The exact nature of the Raphites is unclear, however, they were treated as the spirits or ghosts of the long-dead in texts from across Canaan, in Ugaritic (𐎗𐎔𐎐), Phoenician (𐤓𐤐𐤀𐤌), and Hebrew (רפאים) Canaanite scripts. An editor in the Book of Joshua provided the southern translation of Hinnom (הִנֹם) / Onam (ΟΝΟΜ) for the northern term Refa'im (רְפָאִים). The origin of the word is likely a plural of Hinn (حِنّ), a reference to an ancient extinct type of being that once lived on the Earth in Semitic folklore.

The Hinns continue to be part of the Islamic and Druze religions, although their roles in the religions vary. It is agreed that they are extinct, however, it isn't clear what they were. Many sources describe the hinns and binns as powerful, gigantic primordial creatures, suggesting they were influenced by finding the bones of extinct animals. Conversely, the Revelations of 'Abdullah Al-Sayid

Muhammad Habib claims the Hinns were air creatures, and their enemies the Binns were water creatures, while the medieval Islamic historian al-Tabari claimed they were created from poisonous fire (سموم). In most versions of the stories, they fought in part of a series of wars for control of the earth before the creation of humanity, and most of the ancient species became extinct, including the Hinns. The Greeks interpreted the Raphites as beings like the Gigantes, however, the original term in the Book of Job was likely Rphm, and so the term is imported from the Masoretic text.

2 Codex Vaticanus: apôlia (ΑΠΩΛΕΙΑ). Translation: destruction (or perdition, waste)

• Codex Sinaiticus: ptôchias (ΠΤΩΧΙΑC). Translation: begger

• Aleppo Codex: åbdûn (אַבְדּוֹן). Translation: destruction (or doom, ruin, devastation)

• Leningrad Codex: avaddon (אֲבַדּוֹן). Translation: destruction (or doom, ruin, devastation)

• Targum to Job: åbdānā (אֲבְדָנָא). Translation: destruction (or doom, ruin, devastation)

As Abaddon is considered an archangel of destruction by some Christian groups, and the text is referring to an entity of some kind, the name Abaddon is imported from the Masoretic text.

CHAPTER 26

3 Codex Vaticanus: draconta apostatên (ΔΡΑΚΟΝΤΑ ΑΠΟCΤΑΤΗΝ). Translation: dragon apostate

- Aleppo Codex: nḥš brḥ (נחש ברח). Translation: snake (or magic, divination, enchantment) bolt (or bar)
- Leningrad Codex: nachash bariach (נָחָשׁ בָּרִיחַ). Translation: snake (or magic, divination, enchantment) bolt (or bar)
- Targum to Job: liwyātān dimtîl (לְוְיָתָן דְּמְתִיל). Translation: Leviathan twisted

This seems to be directly related to the previous reference to Cetus, which would seem to confirm that Cetus was a dragon or serpent of some kind, like the Cetus from Perseus mythology, which is likely why the Greeks used that name when transliterating these texts.

4 This entire chapter appears to be about Ba'al Hadad's victory over Yam in the Ugaritic Text's Ba'al Cycle, suggesting that Job, or whoever wrote this chapter, was a worshiper of the Canaanite god of thunder Ba'al Hadad.

Chapter 27

Job further continued with his parable, "The living Lord (the god),[1] who has judged me so, and Resheph, who has made my mind bitter, while my breath is still in me, and the breath of God which remains to me is in my nostrils, my lips will not speak evil words, neither will my mind meditate unrighteous thoughts. Far be it from me that I should justify you till I die, for I will not let go of my innocence, but keeping fast to my righteousness I will by no means let it go, for I am not conscious to myself of having done anything incorrectly. No rather, let my enemies be like the ones overthrown by the ungodly, and they that rise up against me, as the destruction of transgressors. For what is the hope of the ungodly, that he holds to it? Will he indeed trust in the Lord and be saved? Will God hear his prayer? When distress has come on him, has he any confidence before him? Will God hear him as he calls on him? Yet now I will tell you what is in the hand of the Lord, and I will not lie concerning the things which are with Resheph."

"Look, you all know that you are adding vanity to vanity. This is the portion of an ungodly man from the Lord, and the possession of oppressors will come on them from Resheph. If their children are many, they will be slaughtered, and if they grow up, they will beg. They that survive from him will completely perish, and no one will pity their widows. Even if he should gather silver as dirt, and prepare gold as clay. All these things will the righteous gain and the honest will possess his wealth. His house is gone like moths, and like a spider's web. The rich man will lie down, and will not continue, and he has opened his eyes, and he is not. Pains have come on him like water, and the darkness has carried him away by night. A burning wind will catch him, and he will leave, and it will completely drive him out of his place. God will throw trouble on him, and not spare him, and he would not flee out of his hand. He will cause men to flinch their fists against them, and will search him out of his place."

Chapter 27 Notes

1 Codex Vaticanus: zê o cyrios theos (ΖΗΟΚΥΡΙΟCΘΕΟC). Translation: life the lord god

• Codex Sinaiticus: zê o cyrios (ΖΗΟΚΥΡΙΟC). Translation: life the lord

• Codex Alexandrinus: zê cyrios (ΖΗΚΥΡΙΟC). Translation: life lord

• Aleppo Codex: ḥy-ål (חׇי־אֵל). Translation: living god

• Leningrad Codex: chai-el (חַי־אֵל). Translation: living god

• Targum to Job: qayām ĕlāhā (קְיָם אֱלָהָא). Translation: existing (or enduring) god

Chapter 28

[Job continued,] "There is a place for the silver, where it comes from, and a place for the gold, where it is refined from. Iron comes out of the earth, and brass is cut out like stone. He has set a bound to darkness, and he searches out every limit of a stone in darkness, and the shadow of death. There is a cutting off the torrent because of dust so that those who forget the right way are weakened, they are removed from among men. As for the earth, out of it will come bread, and under it has been turned up as it were fire. Her stones are the place of the sapphire, and her dust supplies man with gold. There is a path, the bird has not known it, neither has the eye of the vulture seen it, neither have the sons of the proud trodden it, a lion has not walked on it. He has stretched out his hand on the sharp rock and turned up mountains by the roots, and he has interrupted the whirlpools of rivers, and my eyes have seen every precious thing. He has laid bare the depths of rivers, and has brought his power to light."

"Where has wisdom been discovered? What is the place of knowledge? A mortal has not known its way, neither indeed, has it been discovered among men."

Tiamat[1] said, "It's not in me."

Yam[2] said, "It is not with me."

Chapter 28

"One will not give fine gold instead of it, neither will silver be weighed in exchange for it. Nor can it be compared with the gold of Sauvira, with the precious onyx and sapphire. Gold and crystal will not be equaled to it, neither will vessels of gold be its exchange. Coral and fine pearls will not be mentioned, as you consider wisdom above the most precious things. The gemstones[3] of Kush[4] will not be equal to it. It will not be compared with pure gold. From where then is wisdom found? What kind is the place of understanding? It has escaped the notice of every man, and has been hidden from the birds of the sky."

Abaddon[5] and Mot[6] said, "We have heard the report of it. God has well-ordered the way of it, and he knows the place of it. For he surveys the whole earth under the sky, knowing the things in the earth. All that he has made, and the weight of the winds, the measures of the water. When he made them, he saw this and counted them, and made a way for the pealing of the thunder. Then he saw it and ordered it, and he prepared it and traced it out. He said to man, 'Look, godliness is wisdom, and to abstain from evil is understanding.'"

CHAPTER 28

Chapter 28 Notes

1 Codex Vaticanus: abyssos (ᴀʙʏᴄᴄoᴄ). Translation: abyss

• Aleppo Codex: thům (תהום). Translation: void (abyss, deep)

• Leningrad Codex: tehom (תְהֹום). Translation: void (abyss, deep)

• Targum to Job: tehômā (תְהֹומָא). Translation: void (abyss, deep)

The abyss is a common element in most ancient Middle Eastern religions. In Egyptian beliefs, the abyss was called Nun (𓇴𓈗), meaning "sky waters," and like many of the other religions, this sea was seen as being a cosmic sea, both below the land, and above the sky, and reaching off to infinity. The cosmic sea was an early attempt to envision what is now called outer space, assumed to be composed of freshwater.

The Sumerian name for the primordial waters was deityNammu (𒀭𒇉), however, they also referred to it as abzu (𒀊𒍪), meaning "deep water," and zuab (𒍪𒀊), meaning "water deep." The Greek name abyssou may have been derived from the Sumerian term abzu, however, does not appear to have been imported to Greek thought until the early Iron Age, as the word is not found in the Linear-B script of the Bronze Age.

The Akkadians called the Abyss tâmtu (𒀭𒌈𒌓), which meant "lakes," however, the god that lived in it was replaced with Ia (𒂊𒀀), whose name is believed to be derived from the Sumerian words "praise" (𒂊) and "water" (𒀀). The transliteration of the word as Ia is modern, and if

135

transliterated in Akkadian, the name would have been Šēriš Muú, meaning "praise water."

Ea replaced the earlier Sumerian god ^{deity}Enki (𒂗𒆠), whose name translates as "God Lord Earth." During the Old Babylonian era, Ea was replaced by ^{deity}Nabu (𒀭𒀝), the sun-calf god Marduk's son, and the personification of the planet Mercury in Babylonian cosmology. In Old Babylonian cosmology, the deity of the Abyss tâmtu was ^{deity}Timimat (𒀭𒋼𒀀𒆳), generally transliterated into English a Tiamat. Both tâmtu and Tiamat are recorded in Ugaritic as thm (𐎚𐎅𐎎) and Thmt (𐎚𐎅𐎎𐎚), indicating they were separate concepts in bronze age Canaan. In the book of Habakkuk, written around 612 BC, the goddess was referred to as Tehom (תְהוֹם), presumably in Judahite, the precursor to Classical Hebrew which was written in the Canaanite script.

2 Codex Vaticanus: Thalassa (ΘΑΛΛΑϹϹΑ). Translation: Thalassa (or saltwater, sea)
- Aleppo Codex: ym (יִם). Translation: Yam (or sea, west)
- Leningrad Codex: yam (יִם). Translation: Yam (or sea, west)
- Targum to Job: yamā (יַמָא). Translation: sea

Thalassa was an ancient Greek primordial sea spirit. In ancient Canaanite mythology, the god Yam served the same role. His name is spelled as Ym (𐎊𐎎) in the Ugaritic script and Ym (𐤉𐤌) in the Phoenician script, both of which are identical to the Hebrew spelling, however, his name was spelled as Ymå (𐡉𐡌𐡀) in Aramaic, again indicating the text was in either Ugaritic or Phoenician before being translated into

Aramaic. In the Testament of Judah, the Sea (Θάλασσα) blessed Zebulun, meaning the author(s) of the Testaments of the Twelve Patriarchs still viewed the Sea as sentient in the 2nd century BC.

3 Codex Vaticanus: topazion (ΤΟΠΑΖΙΟΝ). Translation: gemstones (or topaz)

- Aleppo Codex: ptdt (פטדת). Translation: gemstone
- Leningrad Codex: pitdat (פִּטְדָת). Translation: gemstone
- Vetus Latin manuscripts: topadium
- Bohairic manuscripts: topadion (ⲧⲟⲡⲁⲇⲓⲟⲛ)
- Targum to Job: pitlewān (פִּטְלְוָן)

It is unclear which stone the Greeks referred to as topazion (τοπάζιον) as the term was used generically at the time for several gemstones. Likewise, while the Hebrew term, refers to a specific stone, it is unknown today which one.

4 Codex Vaticanus: Aethiopias (ΑΙΘΙΟΠΙΑϹ). Translation: Sudan (or Kush)

- Aleppo Codex: kůš (כוש). Translation: Kush (or Sudan)
- Leningrad Codex: kûš (כּוּשׁ). Translation: Kush (or Sudan)
- Targum to Job: kûš (כּוּשׁ). Translation: Kush (or Sudan)

The term "Aethiopians" was applied to all dark-skinned nations that the Greeks encountered, both in Sub-Saharan Africa and Southern India. The Hebrew term Kush applied to all dark-skinned peoples from Africa and possibly Asia, however, was based on the name of the ancient Nubian Empire based in modern Sudan. The Kushites were well known by the time that the Torah was written, as one of Moses' wives was a Kushite. The land in question was likely Kush (Sudan) and not the modern nation of Ethiopia, as Sudan has always been known as a land of mining. The name of the Nubian tribe is derived from the Nubian word "neb" meaning "gold," and the land continued to be known historically as the "country of metal," until the British Colonial era. Today, Sudanese mines continue to be a major source of gold, as well as quartz gemstones and aluminum-silicate gemstones.

5 Codex Vaticanus: apôlia (ⲀⲦⲦⲰⲖⲈⲓⲀ). Translation: destruction (or perdition, waste)

• Aleppo Codex: âbdûn (אַבְדוּן). Translation: destruction (or doom, ruin, devastation)

• Leningrad Codex: avaddon (אֲבַדּוֹן). Translation: destruction (or doom, ruin, devastation)

• Targum to Job: âbdānā (אָבְדָנָא). Translation: destruction (or doom, ruin, devastation)

As Abaddon is considered an archangel of destruction by some Christian groups, and the text is referring to an entity of some kind, the name Abaddon is copied from the Masoretic text. The exact nature of this being is a matter of much historical debate. The 1st century Christians interpreted him as the angel of death called Abaddôn (Ἀβαδδὼν), who will lead the army of locusts to devour the Earth according to the Apocalypse of John. The word the Greeks used, means essentially "destruction," however, it was also the root of the name Apollo (Ἀπόλλων, Ἀπόλλωνος, Ἀπέλλων, Ἀπείλων, and Ἄπλουν in various dialects), and at other points in the Septuagint, the word Avaddon (אֲבַדּוֹן) was translated as Apollýon (Ἀπολλύων).

Apollo is generally believed by historians today to have been adopted by the Greeks from a Middle Eastern god known by various similar names including the Neshite (Hittite) Apaliunas (𒀪𒉺𒇷𒌋𒈾𒀸), and Hurrian Aplu (𒀀𒅤), both derived from the Akkadian term aplu ᶦˡᵘEllil (𒀀𒅤 𒀭𒂗𒇸), which meant "son of Enlil," which was itself an epitaph of the god Nergal. In the earlier Akkadian era, Nergal seems to have been a god of war and destruction, however, by the Babylonian era he had become a god of plague and destruction, similar to the Apôlia / Avaddon character in Job.

6 Codex Vaticanus: Thanatos (ΘΑΝΑΤΟϹ). Translation: Thanatos (or death, corpse)

- Aleppo Codex: mût (מות). Translation: Mot (or death)
- Leningrad Codex: mavet (מָוֶת). Translation: Mot (or death)
- Targum to Job: malāk môtā (מַלְאָךְ מוֹתָא). Translation: angel Mot (or death)

Mot was the ancient Canaanite god of death, known as Mt (𐎗𐎚) in Ugaritic Canaanite during the Late Bronze Age, and Mt (𐤌𐤕) in Phoenician Canaanite during the Iron Age. He was interpreted as the Israelite messenger (angel) of death in the Classical Era. Thanatos was an ancient Greek god of death and the early Christian angel of death.

Mot (מות), who is speaking, can either be interpreted as the ancient Canaanite god of death or the Second Temple era

Judahite angle of death, depending on when one believes the text has its origin. Mot, the angel of death also appeared in the Book of Habakkuk, while Thanatos appeared in the Testament(s) of Abraham from the 2nd century BC and 3rd century AD. The god Mot fulfilled a position in the Canaanite pantheon similar to Hades and Thanatos in the Greek pantheon. As the name Mot is believed to have been the original name the Greeks translated from, it is restored in this translation, however, all copies of the Septuagint appear to have used Thanatos (Θάνατοσ).

Chapter 29

Job continued his parable, "If only I were like in previous months when God preserved me! When his light shone above my head, and when in his light I walked through darkness. When I steadfastly pursued my ways, when God took care of my house. When I was very fruitful, and my children were around me. When my paths were moistened with butter, and the mountains flowed with milk for me. When I went out early in the city, the seat was placed for me in the streets. The young men saw me and hid themselves, and all the old men stood up. The great men stopped speaking and placed their fingers on their mouths. They who heard me blessed me, and their tongue clung to their throat. For the ear heard, and blessed me, and the eye saw me and turned aside. For I saved the poor out of the hand of the oppressor and helped the fatherless who had no helper."

"Let the blessing of the perishing one come on me. Yes, the mouth of the widow has blessed me. Also, I put on righteousness and clothed myself with judgment like a mantle. I was the eye of the blind and the foot of the lame. I was the father of the helpless, and I searched out the cause which I did not know. I broke the jaw teeth of the unrighteous, I pulled plunder from their teeth. I said, 'My age will continue as the stem of a palm tree, and I will live a long while.' My root was spread out by the water, and the dew would lodge on my crop. My glory was fresh in me, and by bow prospered in his hand. Men heard me and paid attention, and they were silent at my counsel. At my word, they spoke not again, and they were very gland whenever I spoke to them. As the thirsty earth expecting the rain, so they waited for my speech. Were I to laugh at them, they would not believe it, and the light of my face has not failed. I chose out their way, and sat chief, and lived like a king among warriors, as one comforting mourners."

Chapter 30

[Job continued,] "Now the youngest have laughed at me insultingly. Now those whose fathers I considered to be nothing and unworthy to be with my shepherd dogs, take turns insulting me. If only I had the strength of their hands and the full term of life that has been lost. One is childless in lack and famine, such as they that fled but lately the distress and misery of drought. Who surrounds the salt plains on the shore? Who had salt plants for their food, and were dishonorable and of no repute, in lack of every good thing? Who also ate the roots of trees because of great hunger. Thieves have risen up against me, whose houses were the caves of the rocks, who lived under the wild shrubs. They will cry out among the rustling bushes. They are sons of fools and vile men, whose name and glory are quenched from off the earth. But now I am their music, and they have me for a byword."

"They stood apart and abhorred me, and spared not to spit in my face. For he has opened his quiver and afflicted me, they also have thrown off the restraint of my presence. They have risen up against me on the right hand of their offspring, and they have stretched out their foot, and directed against me the ways of their destruction. My paths are ruined, as they have stripped off my clothing, and he has shot at me with his weapons. He has pleaded against me as he wishes, and I am overwhelmed with pain. My pains return on me, my hope is gone like the wind, and my safety is like a cloud. Even now my life will be poured out on me, and days of anguish seize me. By night my bones are confused, and my sinews are relaxed. With great force, my disease has taken hold of my garment, and it has surrounded me like the collar of my coat."

"You have counted me as clay, and my portion in dust and ashes. I have cried to you, but you hear don't me. They stood still and observed me. They attacked me also without mercy, and you have scourged me with a strong hand. You have put me to grief, and have thrown me away from safety. I know that death will destroy me, and the earth is the house appointed for every mortal. If only that I might lay hands on myself, or at least ask another, and he should do this for me. Yet I wept over every helpless man, I groaned when I saw a man in distress. But I, when I waited for good things, look, days of evils came the more on me. My belly boiled, and would not cease, and the days of poverty prevented me. I went mourning without restraint, and I have stood and cried out in the assembly. I have become a brother of monsters and a companion of ostriches. My skin has been greatly blackened, and my bones are burnt with heat. My harp also has been turned into mourning, and my song into my weeping."

Chapter 31

[Job continued,] "I made a covenant with my eyes, and I will not think about a virgin. Now, what portion has God given from above? Is there an inheritance given from Resheph, or from the Highest? Alas! Destruction to the unrighteous, and rejection to those that do iniquity. Will he not see my way, and number all my steps? If I had gone with the insulters, and if too my foot had rushed to deceit, (for I am weighed in a just balance, and the Lord knows my innocence,) if my foot has turned aside out of the way, or if my heart has followed my eye, and if too I have touched gifts with my hands, then let me sow, and let others eat, and let me be uprooted on the earth. If my heart has gone out after another man's wife, and if I laid wait at her doors, then let my wife also please another, and let my children be ashamed. The rage of anger is not to be controlled, in the case of defiling another man's wife. For it is a fire burning on every side, and whoever it attacks, it completely destroys."

"If too I despised the judgment of my slave or my slave-woman when they pleaded with me, what then will I do if the Lord should punish me? If he should ever visit me, can I make an excuse? Were they not also formed as I also was formed in the womb? Yes! We were formed in the same womb. But the helpless did not miss whatever need they had, and I did not cause the eye of the widow to fail."

"If too I ate my food alone and did not give some of it to the orphan, (for I nourished them as a father from my youth and guided them from my mother's womb.) If too I overlooked the naked as he was dying, and did not clothe him, and if the poor did not bless me, and their shoulders were not warmed with the fleece of my lambs, if I lifted my hand against an orphan, trusting that my strength was far superior to his, let them rip my shoulder from the shoulder-blade, and my arm is crushed off from the elbow. For the fear of the Lord constrained me, and I can't continue because of his burden."

"If I made gold my treasure, and if too I trusted in precious stones, and if too I rejoiced when my wealth was abundant, and if too I laid my hand on innumerable treasures, (do we not see the shining sun eclipsed, and the moon waning? They don't have the power to continue.) and if my heart was secretly deceived, and if I have laid my hand on my mouth and kissed it, let this also then be reckoned to me as the greatest iniquity, for I should have lied against the Highest Lord. If too I was glad at the fall of my enemies, and my heart said, 'Aha!' Let then my ear hear my curse, and let me be an example among my people in my affliction."

CHAPTER 31

"If too my slave-women have often said, 'If only we might be satisfied with his flesh, (but I was very kind, for the foreigner did not lodge in need, and my door was opened to everyone that came.) If too having sinned unintentionally, I hid my sin, (for I did not stand in awe of a great multitude, so as not to declare boldly before them,) and if too I permitted a poor man to go out of my door with an empty stomach, (if only I had a judge,) and if I had not been afraid the hand of the Lord, and as to the written charge which I had against anyone, I would place it as a chaplet on my shoulders, and read it. If I did not read it and return it, having taken nothing from the debtor. If at any time the land groaned against me, and if its furrows mourned together, and if I ate its strength alone without price, and if I too grieved the heart of the owner of the soil, by taking anything from him. Then let the nettle come up to me instead of wheat, and a bramble instead of barley."

Job stopped speaking.

Chapter 32

His three friends also stopped talking to Job, for Job was righteous before them. Then Elihu,[1] the son of Barachel, the Buzite,[2] of the families of Ram,[3] of the country of Aysllidi, was enraged and very angry with Job because he justified himself before the Lord. He was also very angry with his three friends because they were not able to answer Job, yet decided he was an ungodly man. Elihu had chosen not to give an answer to Job because the others were older than he was. Elihu saw that there was no answer in the mouths of the three men, and he raged in anger.

Elihu the Buzite the son of Barachel said, "I am younger in age, and you are elder, therefore I kept silent, afraid to tell you my own knowledge. I said, 'It is not time that speaks, though in many years men know wisdom, but there is a spirit in mortals, and the inspiration of Resheph is that which teaches. The long-lived are not necessarily wise, nor do the old know judgment.' Now I say, Hear me, and I will tell you what I know. Listen to my words, for I will speak for you to hear until you will have considered the matter with words, and I will understand as far as you, and, look, there was not one of you that answered Job in his argument, in case you should say, 'We have found that we have been wiser than the Lord.' You have commissioned a man to say such words. They were afraid, they answered no more, and they gave up their speaking. I waited, (for I had not spoken,) because they stood still, and they did not answer."

Elihu continued, "I will again speak, for I am full of words, for the spirit of my belly destroys me. My belly is as a skin of sweet wine, bound up and ready to burst, or like a metalsmith's laboring bellows. I will speak, so I may open my lips and relieve myself. For truly I will not be awed because of man, nor indeed will I be confounded before a mortal. I don't know how to respect people, and if otherwise, even the moths would eat me."

Chapter 32 Notes

1 Codex Vaticanus: Elious (ελιογϲ)

• Dead Sea Scroll 4QJob^a (later in the chapter): ålyhůå (אליהוא)

• Aleppo Codex: ålyhůå (אליהוא).

• Leningrad Codex: Elihu (אֱלִיהֽוּא)

• Targum to Job: ĕlîhû (אֱלִיהוּא)

Elihu is considered by some scholars to be the author of the Book of Job, however, others believe that his speech in chapters 32 through 37 was added later. He is notable in that he was not mentioned at all previously in this book, and disappears after the Lord starts speaking to the other three kings in chapter 38. In the Book of Job, Elihu takes the contrary view to the three kings that are berating Job, and ultimately the Lord punishes them. This is the exact opposite outcome from the Testament of Job, where Elihu is the one berating Job, and punished by the Lord. The Testament of Job contains the Song of Eliphaz, which appears to have been composed before 1000 BC, and claims to have been written by Nahor, the brother of Abraham, and father of Elihu, which seems to be an attempt by the author of the Testament of Job to give it priority over the Book of Job. If Elihu produced the redacted version of Job, adding himself and his opinion to the story, then it was likely when the book was translated into Aramaic.

Elihu's name (אליהו) is based on the words El (אֵל) and Yhů (יהו) which is accepted as the Aramaic form of Yhůh (יהוה), which the Greeks transliterated as Iao (Ιαω), and the Romans transliterated as Iaw. Elihu's name translates as "God is Yhů," however, it is in Aramaic, suggesting he was the Aramaic translator. This would place him in Judea sometime around the time of the reforms of King Hezekiah and King Josiah.

2 Codex Vaticanus: Bouzitês (ΒΟΥΖΙΤΗϹ)
- Septuagint manuscripts N/V: Bouzi (ΒΟΥΖΕΙ)
- Septuagint manuscript 575: Bouzê (βουζ̄λ)

- Aleppo Codex: bůzy (בוזי)
- Leningrad Codex: buzi (בוזי)
- Bohairic manuscripts: Bousitês (Βογϲιτηϲ)
- Sahidic manuscripts: Sōbitês (Ϲⲱⲃⲓⲧⲏϲ)
- Targum to Job: bûzāâ (בוזאה)

In the Torah, Buzites are the descendants of Buz, the son of Nahor, the brother of Abram. They are not known from archaeology, however, if the Torah is correct about them, would have likely been a tribe of shepherds in modern Syria, near the city of Haran.

3 Codex Vaticanus: Ram (ρᴀм)

- Codex Alexandrinus: Rama (ρᴀмᴀ)
- Codex Ephraemi Rescriptus: Aram (ᴀρᴀм)
- Aleppo Codex: rm (רם)
- Leningrad Codex: ram (רָם)
- Sahidic manuscripts: Raman (Pᴀмᴀɴ)
- Targum to Job: åbrāhām (אַבְרְהָם)

There are several people known as Ram in the Septuagint, however, none are associated with Nahor or Elihu, unless this is a reference to Abram, Nahor's brother. Ram was a common name throughout recorded history from Egypt to India.

Chapter 33

Listen to my words Job, and hear my speech. "Look, I have opened my mouth, and my tongue has spoken. My heart will be found pure by my words, and the understanding of my lips will meditate purity. God's breath[1] is that which teaches me. If you can, give me an answer. Wait and debate against me, and I will debate against you. You were formed out of the clay like I was, and so we have been formed out of the same substance. My fear will not terrify you, neither will my hand be heavy on you. But you have said in my ears, (I have heard the voice of your words,) because you say, 'I am pure, not having sinned. I am blameless, for I have not transgressed. Yet he has issued an order against me, and he has reckoned me as an adversary. He has put my foot in the stocks, and has watched all my ways.' How do you say, 'I am righteous, yet he has not listened to me?' as he that is above mortals and eternal."

"You demand, 'Why has he not heard every word of my case?' For when the Lord speaks once, or second time, sending a dream, or in the meditation of the night, (as when a nightmare happens to fall on men while slumbering in the bed,) then he opens the understanding of men. He scares them with such fearful visions to turn a man from unrighteousness, and he delivers his body from a fall. He spares also his mind from death and allows him not to fall in war. Again, he chastens him with sickness in his bed, and the multitude of his bones is benumbed. He will not be able to eat any food, though his mind will desire food until his flesh will be wasted, and he will show his bare bones. His mind also draws near to death, and his life is in Sheol."

"Though there should be a thousand messengers of Mot,[2] not one of them will wound him if he should purpose in his heart to turn to the Lord, and confess to someone his faults, and show his foolishness. He will support him and so he should not die and will restore his body as fresh plaster on a wall, and he will fill his bones with marrow. He will make his flesh tender like that of a babe, and he will restore him among men in his full strength. He will pray to the Lord,[3] and his prayer will be accepted by him. He will enter with a cheerful countenance, with a full expression of praise, for he will render to men their due."

"Though there should be a thousand messengers of Mot, not one of them will wound him if he should purpose in his heart to turn to the Lord, and confess to someone his faults, and show his foolishness. He will support him, and so he does not die, will restore his body like fresh plaster on a wall, and he will fill his bones with marrow. He will make his flesh tender like that of a babe, and he will restore him among men in his full strength. He will pray to the Lord, and his prayer will

be accepted by him. He will enter with a cheerful countenance, with a full expression of praise, for he will
render to men their due."

Chapter 33 Notes

1 Codex Vaticanus: pneuma thion (ΠΝЄΥΜΑΘЄΙΟΝ).
Translation: breath (or spirit, wind) of God

• Septuagint manuscript 575: pneuma de thion (πΝѲυμλ λѕ
θѕιον). Translation: breath (or spirit, wind) of the god

• Aleppo Codex: rûh-âl (אל-רוח). Translation: breath (or
spirit, wind) of God (or El)

• Leningrad Codex: ruach-el (רוּחַ־אֵל). Translation: breath
(or spirit, wind) of God (or El)

• Targum to Job: rûaḥ deĕlāhā (רוּחַ דֶאֱלָהָא). Translation:
wind (or spirit) of god

• Ge'ez Bible: mänifäs goyita (መንፈስ ጎይታ). Translation:
spirit lord

While the word El translates as "god," the word Ruach can
mean wind, spirit, breeze, wraith, spook, ghost, specter,
haunt, air, mind, demon, or soul. This makes understanding
the term Ruach El somewhat more complex. The traditional
Jewish interpretation would be 'God's breath' while the
traditional Christian interpretation is "Holy Ghost." The most
literal translation would be either "wind god" or "ghost god,"
both of which are also traditional translations of the name of
the Babylonian god Ellil's name, "el" meaning "god" and "lil"
meaning "wind" or "ghost." Ruach El is mentioned over 350

times in the Masoretic text, and in almost every book, which implies he continued to be worshiped long after King Josiah's Yahwist reforms.

2 Codex Vaticanus: chilioe angeloe thanatêphoroe (ⲭⲓⲗⲓⲟⲓ ⲁⲅⲅⲉⲗⲟⲓ ⲑⲁⲛⲁⲧⲏⲫⲟⲣⲟⲓ). Translation: thousand messengers (or angles) or Thanatos (or death, corpse)

• Septuagint manuscripts N/V: chilioe angeloe thanatêphoroe ouc apocrinontae autô (ⲭⲓⲗⲓⲟⲓ ⲁⲅⲅⲉⲗⲟⲓ ⲑⲁⲛⲁⲧⲏⲫⲟⲣⲟⲓ ⲟⲩⲕ ⲁⲡⲟⲕⲣⲓⲛⲟⲛⲧⲁⲓ ⲁⲩⲧⲱ). Translation: thousand messengers (or angles) or Thanatos (or death, corpse) not separated (or chosen) of his

• Septuagint manuscript 754: chilioe andres angeloe thanatêphoroe (χϕλιοι ⲁⲛⲁⲣⲟⲥ ⲁⲅⲅⲟⲗⲟⲓ ⲑⲁⲛⲁⲧⲏϐⲟⲣⲟⲓ). Translation: thousand men messengers (or angles) or Thanatos (or death, corpse)

• Septuagint manuscript 254: chilioe angeloe andres thanatêphoroe (χϕλιοι ⲁⲅⲅⲟⲗⲟⲓ ⲁⲛⲁⲣⲟⲥ ⲑⲁⲛⲁⲧⲏϐⲟⲣⲟⲓ). Translation: thousand messengers (or angles) men or Thanatos (or death, corpse)

• Aleppo Codex: mlåk--mlys åḥd mny-ålp (מלאך--מליץ אחד מני-אלף). Translation: ...messenger (or angel). Interpreter (or intercessor) one from a thousand

• Leningrad Codex: mal'ach melitz echad minni-alef (מַלְאָךְ מֵלִיץ אֶחָד מִנִּי־אָלֶף). Translation: Messenger (or angel) interpreter (or intercessor) one from a thousand

CHAPTER 33

• Targum to Job: malăkā hădā peraqlîtā min benê ālep
(מַלְאֲכָא חֲדָא פְּרַקְלִיטָא מִן בְּנֵי אֶלֶף). Translation: messenger one
advocate (or lawyer) from son of a thousand (or Alep)

The two primary codices of the Masoretic texts disagree
slightly here, the Leningrad Codex starts a new sentence
with the word 'messenger,' while the Aleppo Codex treats it
as part of the previous sentence. In either reading the
Masoretic version is unclear, however, it is not clear if the
Greek version was a translation of the Aramaic text or an
interpretation of a confusing sentence. The Masoretic version
does not mention the "angels of death," however, there is no
reason for the Greeks to have invented them either. As
Thanatos was the Greek translation of Mot, the Canaanite
name is restored here, although it is not found in the
Masoretic verse.

3 Codex Vaticanus: cyrion (ΚΥΡΙΟΝ). Translation: lord

• Dead Sea Scroll 4QJobᵃ: ål ål (אֵל אֵל). Translation: god God
(or god El)

• Aleppo Codex: ål-ålůh (אֵל-אֱלוֹהַ). Translation: El-god

• Leningrad Codex: el-elovah (אֵל-אֱלוֹהַ). Translation: El-
god

• Targum to Job: qŏdām ĕlāhā (קֳדָם אֱלָהָא). Translation:
before god

Chapter 34

Elihu continued, "Hear me, you wise men. Listen, you who gain knowledge. The ear tests words, and the mouth tastes food. Let us make the judgment for ourselves. Let us know among ourselves what is right. Job has said, 'I am righteous, the Lord has ignored my judgment. He has erred in my judgment! My wound is severe without my being unrighteousness.' What man is like Job, drinking insults like water? saying, 'I have not sinned, nor committed ungodliness, nor had fellowship with workers of iniquity, to go with the ungodly.' For you should not say, 'There will be no visitation of a man,' when there is a visitation on him from the Lord."

"Therefore hear me you that are wise in heart. Far be it from me to sin before the Lord, or to pervert righteousness before Resheph. Yes, he gives to a man accordingly as each of them does, and in a man's path, he will find him. Do you think that the Lord will make a mistake, or will Resheph who made the earth withhold judgment? Who is he that made the whole world under the sky, and all things within it? For if he would confine, and restrain his spirit with himself, all flesh would die together, and every mortal would return to the earth, from where also he was formed. Pay attention in case he rebukes you. Hear this, listen to the voice of my words. Look then at the one that hates iniquities, and that destroys the wicked, who is fair forever. He is ungodly who says to a king, 'You are a transgressor,' or who says to princes, 'You most ungodly one.' Such a one as would not revere the face of an honorable man, neither knows how to honor to the great, so as that their persons should be respected."

"It will turn out vanity for them, to cry and beg a man, for they dealt unlawfully, the poor being turned aside from their right. He surveys the works of men, and nothing of what they do has escaped him. Neither will there be a place for the workers of iniquity to hide. He will not lay on a man more than is fair, for the Lord looks down on all men and comprehends unknowable things, glorious also and excellent things without number. Who discovers their works, and will bring night on them, and they will be brought low. He quite destroys the ungodly, for they are seen before him. Because they turned aside from the law of God and did not regard his ordinances, to bring before him the cry of the needy, for he will hear the cry of the poor."

"He will give peace, and who will condemn him? He will hide his face, and who will see him? Whether it be done against a nation, or against a man also, causing a hypocrite to be king, because of the waywardness of the people. For there is one that says to Resheph, I have received blessings, and I will not take a pledge, and I will see apart from myself. Show me if I have done unrighteousness, and I will not do it anymore. Will he take vengeance on you for it? Why will you put it far from you? You will choose, and neither will I. Now tell me what you know. Because the wise in heart will say this, and a wise man listens to my words. Job has not spoken with understanding, his words are not uttered with knowledge. How is it you have learned, Job? Don't answer like a foolish one, so we don't add to our sins. Iniquity will be reckoned against us if we speak many words before the Lord."

Chapter 35

Elihu continued, "What is this that you think to be right? Who are you that you have said, 'I am righteous before the Lord?' I will answer you and your three friends. Look up to the sky and observe. Consider the clouds, and how high they are above you. If you have sinned, what will you do? If you have also transgressed, what can you perform? Suppose you are righteous, then what will you give him? What will he receive from your hand? Your ungodliness may affect a man who is like to you, or your righteousness a son of man. They who are oppressed by a multitude will be ready to cry out, and they will call for help because of the great arm."

"But none said, 'Where is the god who made me, and who appoints the guardians of night?[1] Who makes me different from the four-footed beasts of the earth, and from the birds of the sky? They will cry, and no one will listen, even because of the insolence of wicked men. The Lord wants to not see errors, as he is Resheph. He sees those who perform lawless deeds, and he will save me. Do you plead before him? You can praise him, as it is possible to even now. He is not stewing in his anger, nor has he noticed any great trespass. Yet Job vainly opens his mouth in ignorance and he speaks many words."

Chapter 35 Notes

1 Codex Vaticanus: phylacas nycterinas (ϕΥⲗⲗⲕⲁⲥ
ⲚΥⲔⲦⲉⲣⲓⲚⲁⲥ). Translation: guardians (or watchmen) of night

• Aleppo Codex: zmrût blylh (זמרות כלילה). Translation: songstress at night

• Leningrad Codex: zemirovt ballayelah (זְמִרוֹת בַּלַּיְלָה). Translation: songstress at night

• Targum to Job: angelê merômā qŏdāmôy tûšebeḥān belêleyā (אַנְגְלֵי מְרוֹמָא קֳדָמוֹי תּוּשְׁבְּחָן בְּלֵילְיָא). Translation: angels uplifted confront (or meet) settlers nightly

The Hebrew translation is not entirely clear, as zemirovt (זְמִרוֹת) is not a known word. It may be a misspelling of zameret (זָמֶרֶת), which is a female singer. The Greek translators appear to have translated the word shomerim (שׁוֹמְרִים), which means 'guardians' (or watchmen), but is also the root of the name Samaritans, suggesting the term was redacted when the Hebrew translation was made, as the Hasmonean dynasty virtually wiped out the Samaritans, and was most likely responsible for the Hebrew translation of Job. The underlying root of the term Guardians of Night may be related to the name of the star Arcturus, which translates in early Greek as "Guardian of the Bear."

Chapter 36

Elihu further continued, "Bear with me a little while longer, so I may teach you, for there are still words in me. Having brought my knowledge from far away, and according to my own work, I will speak just and true things, and you will not unfairly receive unjust words."

"Know that the Lord will not throw away an innocent man. Being great in strength of wisdom, he will not by any means allow the ungodly to live, and he will grant the judgment of the poor. He will not turn away his eyes from the righteous, but they will be with kings on the throne, and he will establish them in triumph, and they will be exalted. But they that are bound in shackles will be held in cords of poverty. He will recount to them their works, and their transgressions, for such will act with violence."

"He will listen to the righteous, and he has said that they will turn from unrighteousness. If they should hear and serve him, they will spend their days in prosperity, and their years in honor. He will not preserve the ungodly, because they are not willing to know the Lord, and because when reproved they were disobedient. The hypocrites in the heart will array anger against themselves, they will not cry, because he has bound them. Therefore let their mind die in youth, and their life is wounded by messengers of death. They afflicted the weak and helpless, and he will vindicate the judgment of the meek. He has also enticed you out of the mouth of the enemy, there is a deep gulf and a rushing stream beneath it, and your table came down full of fatness."

"Judgment will not fail from the righteous, but there will be anger on the ungodly, because of the ungodliness of the bribes which they received for iniquities. Don't let your mind willingly turn you aside from the petition of the feeble who are in distress. Don't order out all the soldiers at night, so that the people should have to fight instead of them. Pay attention in case you do something wrong, and because of this, you have made choices because of poverty. Look, Resheph will prevail by his strength, as who is as powerful as he is? Who is he that examines his works? Who can say, he has worked injustice? Remember that his works are great beyond those which men have attempted. Every man has seen in himself, how many mortals are wounded."

"Look, Resheph is great, and we will not know him. The number of his years is even infinite. The drops of rain are counted by him and will be poured out in rain to form a cloud. The ancient skies will flow, and the clouds overshadow innumerable mortals. He has fixed time for livestock, and they know the order of rest. Yet by all these things your understanding is not astonished, neither is your mind disturbed in your body. Though one should understand the outspreading of the clouds or the measure of his tent, look he will stretch his bow against him, and he covers the bottom of the sea. Through them, he will judge the nations. He will give food to him who has strength. He has hidden the light in his hands and given orders concerning it to the inter-posing cloud. The Lord will declare concerning this to his friend, but there is a portion also for unrighteousness."

Chapter 37

[Elihu continued,] "At this also my heart is troubled and moved from its place. If you hear a report from the anger of the Lord's fury, discourse will come out of his mouth. He dominates everything under the whole sky, and he lights the extremities of the earth. From him, will come a cry with a loud voice, and he will thunder with the voice of his excellency, yet he will not cause men to die from hearing his voice. Resheph[1] will thunder wonderfully with his voice, for he has done great things which we did not know, commanding the snow to fall on the earth, and the stormy rain, and the storm of the showers from his might. He seals up the hand of every man, that every man may know his own weakness. The wild beasts come in undercover and rest in their lair. Troubles come on out of the secret chambers, and cold from the mountain-tops. From the breath of Resheph, he will send frost, and he guides the water in whatever way he pleases. If a cloud obscures what is precious to him, his light will disperse the cloud. He will carry around the encircling clouds by his governance, to perform their works, whatever he will command them, this has been appointed by him on the earth, whether for correction, or for his land, or if he will find him an object for mercy."

"Listen to this, Job! Stand still and be admonished of the power of the Lord. We know that God has disposed of his works, having made light out of the darkness. He knows the divisions of the clouds, and his signal over-throws the ungodly. But your robe is warm, and there is peace in the land. Did you establish with him the ancient molten mirror?[2] So tell me what will we say to him. Let's stop speaking so much. Do I have a book or a scribe with me, that I may stand and silence the man? The light is not visible to all, it shines far off in the skies, like that which it is from him in the clouds. From Zephon[3] clouds shine like gold. In these are the great glory and honor of Resheph. Another does not find his equal in strength. He that judges justly, do you not think he listens? Therefore, men will fear him, and the also wise in heart will fear him.

Chapter 37 Notes

1 Codex Vaticanus: ischyros (ιϲχγροϲ). Translation: powerful (or strong, mighty)

• Septuagint manuscript 534: crataeos (ϰραταιοϲ). Translation: mighty (or strong)

• Dead Sea Scroll 4QJobᵃ: ôl (ᵓy). Translation: on (or on top of)

• Aleppo Codex: ål (אֵל). Translation: god (or God, strength, to, at, by, not)

• Leningrad Codex: el (אֵל). Translation: god (or God, strength, to, at, by, not)

2 Codex Vaticanus: arasis epichyseôs (ΟΡΛϹΙϹΕΤΤΙΧΥϹΕШϹ).
Translation: seeing (or sight, vision, appearance) molten (or
poured upon)

* Codex Alexandria: arasis epichyseôs (ΟΡΛϹΕΙϹ
ΕΤΤΙϹΧΥϹΕШϹ). Translation: seeing (or sight, vision,
appearance) molten (or poured upon)
* Septuagint manuscript 250: arasis epichyseôs (οῥλσισ
ϭπιχυμᾱτοϲ). Translation: seeing (or sight, vision, appearance)
molten (or poured upon)
* Aleppo Codex: råy mûsq (ראי מוצק). Translation: mirror
solid
* Leningrad Codex: re'i mutzak (רְאִי מוּצָק). Translation:
mirror solid
* Targum to Job: âispaqlaryā sanînā (אִסְפָּקְלַרְיָא סַנִינָא).
Translation: mirror (or windowpane) of Sinai

This reference is generally accepted as a reference to the
"mirror of the sky," a massive mirror that some believed to
cover the sky. At the time mirrors were made from polished
metals, and not silvered glass, like in later periods, which was
why the mirror was referred to as molten.

3 Codex Vaticanus: borra (ΒΟΡΡΛ). Translation: singular
form of 'north' implying a locale
* Aleppo Codex: spûn (צפן). Translation: Zephon (or north)
* Leningrad Codex: tzafon (צָפוֹן). Translation: Zephon (or
north)
* Targum to Job: sippûnā (צִפּוּנָא). Translation: north

CHAPTER 37

Mount Zephon was the holy mountain in the north of Canaan where the temple of the god of thunder Ba'al Hadad was located.

Chapter 38

After Elihu stopped speaking, the Lord asked Job from the whirlwind[1] and clouds, "Who is this that hides counsel from me, and confines words in his heart, and thinks to conceal them from me? Prepare yourself like a man! I will ask you, and you will answer me. Where were you when I created the Earth? Tell me now, if you know. Who set the measures of it? Do you know? Who stretched a line on it? On what are its rings fastened? Who is it that laid the cornerstone of it? When the stars were made, all my messengers praised me with a loud voice. I locked up the sea with gates, when it rushed out, coming forth out of its mother's womb. I made its clothing a cloud and surrounded it in mist. I set bounds to it, surrounding it with bars and gates. I said to it, 'You have come this far, but you will go no farther, and your waves will be confined within you.'"

"Did I order the morning light in your time, and Shahar[2] saw his appointed place to grab hold of the extremities of the earth, and to throw out the ungodly out of it? Did you take clay from the ground, form a living creature on the earth, and set within it the power of speech? Have you removed the light from the ungodly, and crushed the arm of the proud? Have you gone to the source of the sea, and walked through the abyss? Do the gates of Mot[3] open to you in fear? Did the porters of Sheol quake when they saw you? Have you been taught about the width of everything under the sky? Tell me now, what is the extent of it? In what kind of land does the light live, and where is the place of darkness? Bring me to their borders, if also you know their paths."

"I know when you were born, at that time, and the number of your years is great, but have you gone to the vault of snow? Have you seen the vault of hail? Is there a reserve for you, for the time of wars and battle against your enemies? Where does the frost come from? Is the South Wind dispersed over everything under the sky? Who planned a path of the violent rain, and the path for the thunders to rain on the empty wilderness, to feed the wild and uninhabited land, and cause it to grow crops of green plants? Who is the rain's father? Who has generated the drops of dew? Who gives birth to the ice? Who has produced the sleet in the sky which falls like flowing water? Who has terrified the face of the ungodly?"

"Do you know the bonds of Pleiades,[4] and have you opened the belt of Orion?[5] Will you reveal constellations[6] in their seasons, and Hyades[7] with his rays? Will you guide them? Do you know the changes in the sky or all the events that take place under the sky? Will you call a cloud with your voice, and will it obey you with a violent rainstorm? Will you send lightning, and they will come and say to you, 'What is it?'"

"Who has given to women skill in weaving, or knowledge of embroidery? Who is he that has the wisdom to count the clouds, and who brought the sky to the earth? It is spread out over dusty earth, and I have cemented it as one cut stone to another. Will you hunt the prey for the lions and satisfy the desires of the dragons? They lay afraid in their lairs, and wait crouched in the forest. Who has prepared food for the raven? It's young ones who wander and beg to the Lord, in search of food."

Chapter 38 Notes

1 Codex Vaticanus: laelapos (ΛΑΙΛΑΠΟϹ). Translation: whirlwind (or tornado)

- Aleppo Codex: mnhsôrh [mn hsôrh] (מנהסערה [מן הסערה]). Translation: part of the storm [from the storm]

- Leningrad Codex: min hasse'arah [min hasse'arah] (מִן הַסְּעָרָה [מִן ו הַסְּעָרָה]). Translation: from the storm [from. the storm]

- Targum to Job: min ôalôlā (מִן עַלְעוֹלָא). Translation: from the revoloving (or spinning)

2 Codex Vaticanus: eôsphoros (ⲉⲱⲥⲫⲟⲣⲟⲥ). Translation: Heosphorus

- Septuagint manuscript 251: phôsphoros (ⲫⲟⲟⲥⲫⲟⲣⲟⲥ).

Translation: light bringer (or torch bearer)

- Aleppo Codex: boker yd'th shchr [yidda'tah hashachar] (כֶר ידעתה שחר [ידעת השחר]). Translation: morning to know Shahar [to know the dawn]

- Leningrad Codex: bōqer yiddaôtâ k šahar k [yiddaôtā q haššahar q] (בֶּקֶר ידעתה שחר [וְיִדְעָתָה הַשָּׁחַר]). Translation: morning to know Shahar [to know the dawn]

- Targum to Job: min ôalôlā desaôãrā (מִן עַלְעוֹלָא דְצַעֲרָא).

Translation: from misfortune of pain

This is another example of the Greeks translating the name Shahar as Heosphorus. The Masoretic version of Job includes both a direct translation of 'morning to know Shahar' and the interpretation of "morning to know the dawn," confirming that Shahar was in the text the Hebrew scribes translated. However, Shahar was the god of dawn, like the Egyptian god Khepri, Greek Titaness Eos, and Roman goddess Aurora. The Canaanite equivalent of Heosphorus was Aziz, also called Helel in Hebrew. As the Greeks appear to have translated Shahar as Heosphorus consistently in the Book of Job, the name Shahar is restored in this translation.

3 Codex Vaticanus: pylae thanatou (ⲡⲨⲖⲀⲒ ⲐⲀⲚⲀⲦⲞⲨ). Translation: gates (or doors, entrances, portals) of Thanatos (or death, corpse)

- Aleppo Codex: šôry-mŭt (שַׁעֲרֵי-מָוֶת). Translation: gateway of Mot (or death)
  - Leningrad Codex: sha'arei-mavet (שַׁעֲרֵי-מָוֶת). Translation: gateway of Mot (or death)
    - Targum to Job: maôalanê môtā (מַעֲלָנֵי מוֹתָא). Translation: finger of death

4 Codex Vaticanus: desmon Pliados (ΔΕϹΜΟΝ ΠΛΕΙΑΔΟϹ). Translation: bond (or fetter, collar, bondage, imprisonment, spell, heart) of the Pleiades

- Aleppo Codex: môdnŭt kymh (מַעֲדַנּוֹת כִּימָה). Translation: bond (or influence) of the Pleiades
  - Leningrad Codex: ma'adannovt kimah (מַעֲדַנּוֹת כִּימָה). Translation: bond (or influence) of the Pleiades
    - Targum to Job: šêrê kîmetā (שֵׁירֵי כִּימְתָא). Translation: ring (or cuff, shackle) of Pleiades

5 Codex Vaticanus: Ôriônos (ωριωΝΟϹ) Translation: Orion
- Aleppo Codex: ksyl (כְּסִיל). Translation: Orion (or fool)
- Leningrad Codex: ksl (כְּסִיל). Translation: Orion (or fool)
- Targum to Job: niplā (נְפִלָא). Translation: Npylå (or Orion)

The name in the Aramaic text was Npylå (ܢܦܝܠܐ), where the Nephilim (Orionids) fell from each October. The Orionids are a meteor shower that happens each year, between October 2 and November 7, as the Earth passes through the debris left by Halley's Comet. Peaks of 70 meteors a minute have been recorded, and these meteors fall from the region of the sky where Orion's upstretched arm is located.

CHAPTER 38

6 Codex Vaticanus: mazourôth (ᴍ**ᴀᴢ**ᴏ**ʏ**ᴩ**ω**ө)

* Septuagint manuscript 130: nazourôth (ɴ**ᴀᴢ**ᴏᴜβ**ꝏ**θ)

* Aleppo Codex: mzrût (מזרות)

* Leningrad Codex: mazzarot (מַזָּרוֹת)

* Bohairic manuscripts: masourōt (ᴍᴀ**ᴄ**ᴏʏᴩ**ω**ᴛ)

* Targum to Job: mazālayā (מַזְלַיָּא). Translation: constellation within the Zodiac

The term mazzarot (מַזָּרוֹת) is often generally as "zodiac" or "constellations," and is derived from the Neo-Babylonian mazraåtu (𒂍𒈨𒌷𒀀𒈨), meaning "mansions" or "manors." It may have begun as a reference to the Egyptian decans, 36 small constellations spread around the ecliptic, which the Egyptians used to tell the time at night. These decans were influential in the development of Asian astrology, and Indian astrology continues to use versions of them.

7 Codex Vaticanus: esperon (**ᴇ**ᴄ**ᴛᴛ**ᴇᴩ**ᴏɴ**). Translation: Hesperus

* Aleppo Codex: ôyš (עיש). Translation: Wagon (or Ursa Minor)

* Leningrad Codex: ayish (עַיִשׁ). Translation: Wagon (or Ursa Minor)

* Targum to Job: zagtā al eprāhāhā (זַגְתָּא עַל אֶפְרְחָהָא). Translation: hen and her chicks

This is a significant difference between the Greek and Hebrew Books of Job. The Wagon (עַיִשׁ) in the Masoretic Text is a reference to Ursa Minor in the Babylonian star-charts, which the Phoenicians, and then Greeks used for navigation. Between 1800 BC and 400 AD, there was no specific star near the celestial north pole, and groups of stars closest to the north pole were collectively used for navigation. The Greeks originally called the constellation the Phoenician Bear, after learning how to navigate by it from the Canaanites. However, the Greeks would not have translated the Wagon as the Evening Star, as they had studied Babylonian astronomy, and there was a Greek word for 'wagon.' As the spelling of the Hebrew name in the Masoretic version of this verse, ayish (עַיִשׁ), is different from the other references to the Wagon found in Job, ash (עָשׁ), some rabbis have proposed it is a different star, specifically the Hyades star cluster in Taurus has been proposed, as the Pleiades and Hyades have been treated as a pair of star clusters since ancient times, known as the Golden Gate of the Ecliptic, as all planets orbiting the sun appear to pass between these star-clusters during their orbits. It is worth noting that the Hyades star cluster would have been the evening stars during the Northern vernal equinox around 2000 BC, which supports both the Rabbinical interpretation of the name Ayish, and the Greek translation of Hesperus, and therefore, the name Hyades is used in this translation.

Chapter 39

[The Lord continued,] "Say if you know the time when the wild goats will come out of the rocks and if you have predicted the calving of the donkeys, and if you have counted the full months of their being with young, and if you have relieved their labor, and have reared their young without fear. Will you lessen their labor? Their young will break out, and they will be multiplied with offspring. Their young will go away, and will not return to them. Who is he that sent out the wild donkey? Who released him? I made his home the wilderness, and the salt lands his cover. He laughs to mock the multitude in the city and does not hear the call of the tax collector. He will survey the mountains as his pasture, and he searches for everything green."

"Will the rhinoceros[1] be willing to serve you, or to lie down at your manger? Will you bind the rhinoceros with a yoke, and will he plow furrows for you in the plain? Do you trust the rhinoceros because of his great strength? Will you commit your work to him? Will you believe that he will return to your seed, and bring it to your threshing floor?"

"The peacock has a beautiful tail. If the stork and the ostrich conceive, she will leave her eggs in the ground, and warm them in the dirt, and has forgotten that the foot will scatter them, and the wild beasts of the field trample them. She has hardened against her young ones and does not concern herself. She labors in vain without fear. For God has withheld wisdom from her, and not given her a portion in understanding. In her season, she will lift herself high, and she will mock the horse and his rider."

"Have you given the horse strength, and collar his neck with fear? Have you clad him in perfect armor, and made his breast glorious with courage? He ruts exulting in the plain and goes out in strength to the plain. He laughs to mock a king when he meets him, and will by no means turn to run from the sword. The bow and sword resound against him, and his rage will swallow up the ground, and he will not believe until the trumpet sounds. When the trumpet sounds, he says, 'Bravo!' and from far away he smells as war and prances and neighs."

"Does the hawk remain steady by your wisdom, having spread out her wings unmoved, looking towards the region of the south? Does the eagle rise at your command, and the vulture remains sitting over his nest, on a crag of a rock, and in a hidden place? He searches for food from there, his eyes seeing from far away. His young ones roll themselves in blood, and wherever a carcass is near they are found."

CHAPTER 39

Lord the god² asked Job, "Will anyone pervert judgment with Resheph? He who debates God,³ let him answer."

Job answered the Lord, "Why do I still beg? Being rebuked even while debating the Lord? Hearing such things, when I am nothing, and what will I answer to these arguments? I will lay my hand on my mouth. I have spoken once, but I will not do so a second time."

Chapter 39 Notes

1 Codex Vaticanus: monocerôs (ⲘⲞⲚⲞⲔⲈⲢⲱⲤ). Translation: unicorn (or narwhal)

* Septuagint manuscript 261: atrapelos (ⲀⲧⲢⲀⲡⲟ̔Ⲗⲟⲥ)

* Aleppo Codex: rym (רים). Translation: wild buffalo (in Aramaic)

* Leningrad Codex: reim (רֵים). Translation: wild buffalo (in Aramaic)

* Sahidic manuscripts: monokurōs (ⲘⲞⲚⲞⲔ ⲨⲢⲱⲥ)

* Targum to Job: rêmānā (רֵימָנָא). Translation: pomegranate

The Greek term monocerôs, which means single-horn, was a legendary animal from India, believed to have first been mentioned under its Greek name in Aeschylus' writing in the 5ᵗʰ century BC, which is accepted as a description of an Asian rhinoceros, which, unlike their African counterparts, only have one horn.

The word rym (רים) is accepted as the Aramaic word for onyx or wild buffalo, which is known as the råm (ראם) in Hebrew, and riåm (رِئْم) in Arabic. It was also recorded in earlier languages as the rimu (𒊑𒈬) in Akkadian Cuneiform, and the rům (𒀭𒉡) in Ugaritic Canaanite.

It is unclear why the Greeks would have translated "oryx" as "unicorn," as the Ancient Greek word for "oryx" was aryx (ὄρυξ), from which many European languages adopted the name. As the word found in the Masoretic version of Job appears to be the Aramaic name transliterated into the Hebrew script, the Aramaic word was used in the source texts the Hebrew translators used, and therefore, should have been in the Aramaic text the Greeks translated. There are some differences in the Greek and Hebrew versions of Job that may have originated in two separate Aramaic versions of Job, and therefore, the Greeks may have seen a word other than rym (𐤓𐤉𐤌) in the text they translated.

2 Codex Vaticanus: cyrios o theos (ΚΥΡΙΟϹΟΘΕΟϹ). Translation: lord the god
- Aleppo Codex: Yhůh (יהוה)
- Leningrad Codex: Yehvah (יְהֹוָה)
- Targum to Job: yeyā (??). Translation: Yhů

3 Codex Vaticanus: theon (ΘΕΟΝ). Translation: god
- Aleppo Codex: ålůh (אלוה). Translation: god
- Leningrad Codex: eloah (אֱלֹוֹהַ). Translation: god

Chapter 40

The Lord continued to speak to Job out of the cloud,[1] and said, "Prepare yourself like a man! I will ask you, and you will answer me. Do not ignore my judgment, and do you think that I have dealt with you in a way that you might not think of as righteous? Have you an arm like the Lord's? Do you thunder with a voice like his? Assume now a lofty bearing and power, and clothe yourself with glory and honor. Send out messengers in anger, and humiliate the violent ones, and humiliate the proud man, and immediately consume the ungodly. Hide them together in the earth, and fill their faces with shame. Then I will confess that your hand can save you."

"But now look at the Behemoth.[2] See now, its strength is in its loins, and its strength is in the navel of its belly. It waved its tail like a cypress, and its nerves were wrapped together. Its sides are sides brass, and its backbone is like cast iron. This is the chief creation of the Lord,[3] made for his messengers to play with. When it approaches a high mountain, it brings tranquility to the quadrupeds in Tartarus.[4] It lies under trees of every kind, and next to papyrus, reeds, and bulrush. The great trees shadow it with their branches, as do the bushes of the field. If there is a flood, it will not notice it. It knows that Jordan will rush up past it mouth. Yet if one catches sight of it, one can catch it with a rope and pierce it nose."

"But will you catch Leviathan[5] with a hook, and put a halter about his nose? Will you fasten a ring in his nostril, and trap his lips with a clasp? Will he beg you softly, with the voice of a suppliant? Will he make a covenant with you? Will you take him as a perpetual slave? Will you play with him like a bird, or trap him like a sparrow for a child? Do the nations feed on him, and share him with the Canaanites?[6] All the ships coming together would not be able to carry just the skin from his tail, and they would not be able to carry his head in the vessels. But if you lay your hand on him once, remember the war is waged through his mouth, and not let it be done anymore."

Chapter 40 Notes

1 Codex Vaticanus: nephôn (ΝЄⲫⲱΝ). Translation: smog (or nebula)

• Septuagint manuscripts N/V: nephous (ΝЄⲫⲞⲨⲥ). Translation: cloud (or mist, smog)

• Septuagint manuscript 248: nephelês (νϬⲫϬⲗⲏⲥ).

Translation: cloud (or mass)

• Aleppo Codex: mnsôrh [mn sôrh] (מנסערה [מן סערה]).

Translation: from agitation (or turbulence) [from storm]

• Leningrad Codex: mn s'rh [min se'arah] (מ סערה [מֶן סְעָרָה]).

Translation: from storm [from storm]

- Targum to Job: min alôlîtā (מִן עַלְעוֹלִיתָא). Translation: from the whirlwind (or hurricane, spinning)

2 Codex Vaticanus: thêria (ⲐⲎ ⲢⲓⲀ). Translation: beasts (or brutes, predators, wild animals)
- Aleppo Codex: bhmût (בהמות)
- Leningrad Codex: behēmôt (בְּהֵמוֹת)
- Peshitta: bhmût (ܒܗܡܘܬ)
- Targum to Job: beîrayā (בְּעִירַיָא). Translation: beast of burden

The Greeks clearly did not know what animal the word behemoth represented, and so used the generic term "beasts." This translation of "beasts" (בעירא) was also used the Aramaic Targum, which was created in the 1st century BC to interpret the Hebrew translation of the Israelite holy books to the Aramaic speaking Judeans. The term itself is accepted as being Aramaic, and a plural form of bhmû (עתלך), however, that word is not found in any known Aramaic text. The Syriac Christian translation found in the Peshitta, the Syriac Orthodox Bible, uses the identical spelling of bhmût (ܒܗܡܘܬ) in the later Syriac script, supporting the original Aramaic term as having been the plural form of bhmw. The pre-Christian sections of the Peshitta were, according to the Syrian scholars that translated it, based on the ancient Aramaic version of the texts that predated the Hebrew translations of the Torah and Tanakh. While this is not accepted by all scholars, it is clear that the Syriac and Hebrew terms are derived from an Aramaic word or at least a loanword used in

Aramaic by the author. The theory most accepted at this time by linguists is that it is an Aramaic transliteration of the Ancient Egyptian word påîhmŭ (𒀭𒈗𒄩𒈬), meaning "water ox," and therefore, the Book of Job appears to have at one point been translated into in Egyptian.

The Ancient Egyptians had several names for "hippopotamus," however, generally called it a ḥåb (𒀭𒈗𒄩), and therefore, while the Book of Job may have been written in Egyptian hieroglyphs, it probably wasn't written in the Egyptian language, suggesting it was written in Canaan during the Middle Kingdom, or in northern Egypt during the Canaanite (13ᵗʰ) dynasty or Hyksos (14ᵗʰ) dynasty. In any event, sometime before the New Kingdom Era, when the term ss yåŭr (𐤒𐤉𐤀𐤓 𐤕𐤕), meaning "horse of the Nile," was adopted by the Canaanites as a name for the hippopotamus. The Canaanite term is virtually identical to the two Egyptian words ssm (𒀭𒈗𒄩), meaning "horse," and îtrŭ (𒀭𒈗𒄩), meaning "great river," suggesting the term was also used in Late Egyptian, however, it is undocumented before the Classical Era.

This term was later imported to Median and Persian as "aspa ap" from the Avestan words apsa (سربوسد), meaning "horse," and ap (سو), meaning "water," and continues today in the Persian term for hippopotamus, asb-e âbi (اسـب آبی). The Persian term appears to have been the basis of the Greek and Arabic terms hippopotamos (ἱπποπόταμος) and faras nahr (فرس نهر), both of which combine the words for "horse" and "river." A similar term is also used in Coptic, the Classical Era form of Egyptian, as htho ior (ⲟⲑⲟ ⲓⲟⲣ), which translates as "Nile horse."

In this case, the verse seems to be referring both to actual hippopotamuses that lay in marshes, and also the Egyptian asterism of Taweret, named after a goddess who combined the forms of a hippopotamus and a crocodile. Taweret was the other asterism in the far north. Taweret was a very ancient goddess whose worship was widespread throughout Egypt, Nubia, Canaan, and the Minoan civilization. This common Egyptian form was depicted as an upright walking hippopotamus with a long crocodile tale. She was described in the Egyptian Book of Day and Night from the late Bronze Age as the guardian of the leg of Sutekh, their name for the Big Dipper. The Hyksos dynasty, which had ruled both Egypt and Canaan during the middle Bronze Age, had equated the Egyptian god Sutekh, with the Canaanite god Seth, and the Amorite god Hadad, collectively known as Ba'al, meaning "Lord." As a northern asterism, Taweret was at the opposite end of the sky from the Leviathan (Yam, Cetus), which was on the southern horizon, explaining the opposing yet coupled relationships of the beings in the texts that mention them.

Whatever the word Behemoth represented to the authors, it continued to be used in Hebrew and Aramaic literature until at least 200 BC. In the Book of Enoch, Behemoth was reported to live in a desert east of Eden, which may have been a metaphor, or a reference to an eastern desert. This may have been an ancient reference to dinosaur bones being dug up in the Gobi Desert. Ancient texts such as the

Shennong Bencaojing prescribe the use of 'dragon bones' in Chinese medicine, which were no doubt excavated from the Gobi Desert, as they are today. Although it is unclear when King Shennong lived, his life is traditionally dated to 2437 BC. The medical text attributed to him, the Shennong Bencaojing, has existed since 200 AD at the latest but is believed to date back to before the time of Qin Shi Huang circa 220 BC.

The probable link between the Ancient Egyptian word for 'water buffalo' and the Aramaic term "bhmŭ" was worked out in the Late-Classical Era, and therefore influenced the languages within the Byzantine and Russian Empires, resulting in the words for "hippopotamus" being derived from behemoth in many languages, including Armenian (բեհեմօթ), Azerbaijani (begemot), Belarusian (бегемо́т), Bulgarian (бегемо́т), Chuvash (бегемот), Georgian (ბეჰემოთი), Hebrew (בְּהֵמוֹת), Kazakh (бегемот), Kyrgyz (бегемот), Latvian (behemots), Lithuanian (begemotas), Ossetian (бегемот), Russian (бегемо́т), Tajik (баҳмут), Turkmen (begemot), Ukrainian (бегемо́т), Uyghur (بېگېموت), and Uzbek (begemot). In some of these languages, the term is now considered dated and has been replaced with words based on the Greek word hippopotamos (ἱπποπόταμος).

3 Codex Vaticanus: tout estin archê plasmatos cyriou (ΤΟΥΤ ΕϹΤΙΝ ΑΡΧΗ ΠΛΑϹΜΑΤΟϹ ΚΥΡΙΟΥ). Translation: this (or here) is the principal (or main, greatest) creation of lord

• Septuagint manuscript 336: touto estin archê plasmatos cyriou (τουτο ϵστιν αϝχϧ πλαϝϩϻατοσ ᴌυϼϕου). Translation:

this (or here) is the principal (or main, greatest) creation of lord

• Septuagint manuscript 337: tout' estin archê plasmatos cyriou theou (τουτ ϭοτιɴ ΔϷχʰ πλαⱴϭμΔτοϭ ʟυϷϸου θϭου).

Translation: this (or here) is the principal (or main, greatest) creation of lord God

• Aleppo Codex: hûâ râšyt drky-âl (**הוא ראשית דרכי-אל**). Translation: he (or it) is the first (or beginning, first-fruit, principle) of the path (or road) of God (or El)

• Leningrad Codex: hu reshit darchei-el (הוּא רֵאשִׁית דְּרְכֵי-אֵל). Translation: he (or it) is the first (or beginning, first-fruit, principle) of the path (or road) of God (or El)

• Targum to Job: hû šerûyâ ôrehâtêh deëlâhâ (הוּא שְׁרוּיָא אוֹרְחָתֵיהּ דֶאֱלָהָא). Translation: he (or it) ruled the path (or road) of God

4 Codex Vaticanus: tetraposin en tô tartarô (ΤΕΤΡΔΠΟϲιɴ ЄN ΤѡΤΔΡΤΔΡѡ). Translation: quadrupeds in (or at, on) the Tartarus

• Septuagint manuscripts N/V: tetraposin en tô tartarô (ΤΕΤΡΔΠΟϲιɴ ЄN ΤѡΤΔΡѡ). Translation: quadrupeds in (or at, on) the Taro

• Septuagint manuscript 68: tetraposin en tôtetartô (τϭτϷΔπΟϭιɴ ϭɴ τοοτϭτΔϷτοο). Translation: quadrupeds in (or at, on) the Totetarto

• Aleppo Codex: ḥyt hšdh (**חית השדה**). Translation: lifeforms (or living things) the field (or demon, she-devil)

• Leningrad Codex: chayyat hassadeh (חַיַת הַשָּׂדֶה). Translation: lifeforms (or living things) the field (or demon, she-devil)

• Targum to Job: ḥêwat bārā (חֵיוַת בָּרָא). Translation: animal of the forest

5 Codex Vaticanus: draconta (ΔΡΑΚΟΝΤΑ). Translation: dragon

• Aleppo Codex: lůytn (לְוִיתָן). Translation: Leviathan, Lotan

• Leningrad Codex: livyatan (לִוְיָתָן). Translation: Leviathan

The Greeks generally translated Leviathan as Cetus, due to the association of the two constellations. In this case, the text was interpreted as referring to a literal creature that was living somewhere, however, the description that follows sounds more like the description of a steam-powered ship than a living creature.

6 Codex Vaticanus: Phoenicôn (ΦΟΙΝΙΚΩΝ) Translation: Phoenicians (or Canaanites)

• Aleppo Codex: knônym (כנענים). Translation: Canaanites (or Phoenicians)

• Leningrad Codex: kena'anim (כְּנַעֲנִים). Translation: Canaanites (or Phoenicians)

Canaanite and Phoenician were two terms that both referred to the same people. The term Canaanite appears to be the Akkadian name, based on the words "red people," while the term Phoenician appears to be derived from the Egyptian words "purple people." The indigenous name of the people of

CHAPTER 40

Canaan/Phoenicia was likely Adam, which means both "red" and "man," in Canaanite.

Chapter 41

[The Lord continued,] "Have you not seen him? Have you not wondered at the things said of him? Are you not afraid because preparations have been made by me? Who is there that resists me? Who will resist me and survive, since the whole world under the sky is mine? I will not be silent because of him, though because of his power, one will pity his antagonist. Who will open the face of his garment? Who can enter within the fold of his breastplate? Who will open the doors of his face? Terror is around his teeth. His insides are bronze plates with a texture like schist stone, one clings fast to another, and the air can't come between them. They will remain united each to the other, and they are closely joined, and can't be separated."

"When he starts sneezing, a light shines, and his eyes shine like the morning star. Out of his mouth comes something like burning lamps, and the sacrificial fires are thrown around. Out of his nostrils comes the smoke of a furnace burning with the fire of coals. His breath is live coals, and a flame comes out of his mouth. Power is living in his neck, and before him, streams destruction.[1] The flesh of his body is joined together, poured onto him, and he will not be moved. His heart is firm as a stone, and it stands like an unyielding anvil. When he turns, he causes terror to the four-footed wild beasts which run on the earth. If spears should come against him, they have no effect, the spear or the breastplate. He considers iron like chaff and brass like rotten wood. A brass bow will not injure him, and he sees a slinger as grass, mauls are counted as stubble, and he laughs to mock the waving of the firebrand. His lair is sharp points and all the sea of gold under him like an immense clay. He makes the abyss[2] boil like a bronze cauldron, and he regards the sea like a pot of ointment, and Tartarus in the Abyss like a captive. He considers the Abyss as his territory. There is nothing on the earth like him, created to be played with by my messengers. He sees everything high, and he is the king of all that is in the water."

Chapter 41 Notes

1 Codex Vaticanus: emprosthen autou trechi apôlia (ЄМΠΡΟCΘЄΝ ΑΥΤΟΥ ΤΡЄΧЄΙ ΑΠΩΛЄΙΑ) Translation: before him runs (or flees, moves quickly, flows, steams) destruction (or loss)

- Aleppo Codex: lpnyŭ tdŭṣ dåbh (**לפניו תדוץ דאבה**).

Translation: in front of him springs (or dances, leaps) worry

- Leningrad Codex: lefanav tadutz de'avah (לְפָנָיו תָּדוּץ דְּאָבָה). Translation: in front of him springs (or dances, leaps) worry

2 Codex Vaticanus: abysson (ⲀⲂⲨⳚⳖⲞⲚ) Translation: abyss

- Septuagint manuscripts N/V: thalassan (ⲐⲀⳞⳞⲀⳚⳚⲀⲚ). Translation: sea
- Aleppo Codex: mṣûlh (מְצוּלה). Translation: deep water
- Leningrad Codex: mẹtzulah (מְצוּלָה). Translation: deep water
- Targum to Job: meṣûletā (מְצוּלְתָא). Translation: depths

Chapter 42

Then Job answered the Lord, "I know that you can do all things, and nothing is impossible for you. For who is he that hides counsel from you? Who holds back his words, and thinks to hide them from you? Who will tell me what I did not know, great and wonderful things which I did not understand? Nevertheless, hear me, the Lord, so I may also speak, and I will ask you, and you answer me. I have heard reports of you before, but now my eyes have seen you. Therefore, I see myself as vile and have fainted. I consider myself dust and ashes."

After the Lord had spoken all these words to Job, the Lord said to Eliphaz the Temanite, "You have sinned, and your two friends, for you have not said anything honest before me like my servant Job. Now then take seven bulls, and seven rams, and go to my servant Job, and he will offer a burnt offering for you. My servant Job will pray for you, for I will only accept him. If not for him, I would have murdered you all, as you have not spoken the truth against my servant Job."

Eliphaz the Temanite, Bildad the Shuhite, and Zophar the Minaean went and did as the Lord commanded them, and he pardoned their sin for the sake of Job. The Lord blessed Job, and when he prayed also for his friends, he forgave them their sins, and the Lord gave Job twice as much, double what he had before. All his brothers and his sisters heard all that had happened to him, and they came to him, and so did all that had known him from before, and they ate and drank with him, and comforted him over all the evil that the Lord[1] had done to him. Each one gave him a lamb and four drachmas' weight of gold and silver.[2] The Lord[3] blessed the latter days of Job, more than the beginning, and his livestock were fourteen thousand sheep, six thousand camels, a thousand yoke of oxen, a thousand donkeys in the pastures."

Seven sons and three daughters were born to him. He called the first Yemimah,[4] and the second Cassia,[5] and the third Cornucopia.[6] There were none found more beautiful than the daughters of Job in all the world, and their father gave them an inheritance among their brothers. Job lived after his affliction a hundred and seventy years, and all the years he lived were two hundred and forty. Job saw his sons and his grandsons, and the fourth generation. Job died an old man and full of days, and it is written that he will rise again with those who the Lord resurrects.

Chapter 42 Notes

1 Codex Vaticanus: cyrios (ΚΥΡΙΟΣ). Translation: lord
- Papyrus Oxyrhynchus 3522 (LXX 857): yhůh (𐤉𐤄𐤅𐤄)

CHAPTER 42

- Aleppo Codex: yhŭh (**יהוה**)
- Leningrad Codex: yehvah (יְהֹוָה)
- Targum to Job: yeyā (יְיָ). Translation: Yhŭ

Papyrus Oxyrhynchus 3522 dates to the 1st century AD. It is a group of fragments of what appears to be the Septuagint's Job with the word Lord (Κύριοσ) replaced with Yhŭh (𐤉𐤄𐤅𐤄) in the Canaanite script, confirming that the original Greek translation of Job did not include the name Iaw (Ιαω).

2 Codex Vaticanus: edôcen de autô hecastos amnada mian cae tetradrachmon chrysoun asêmon (ЄΔѠΚЄΝ ΔЄ ΑΥΤѠ ЄΚΑϹΤΟϹ ΑΜΝΑΔΑ ΜΙΑΝ ΚΑΙΤЄΤΡΑΔΡΑΧΜΟΝ ΧΡΥϹΟΥΝ ΑϹΗΜΟΝ). Translation: gave and him each ewe-lamb one and four drachmas golden sliver (or plate)

- Aleppo Codex: ŭytnŭ-lŭ åyš qšyth åht ŭåyš nzm zhb åhd (וַיִּתְּנוּ־לוֹ אִישׁ קְשִׂיטָה אַחַת וְאִישׁ נֶזֶם זָהָב אֶחָד). Translation: and gave him man k'sitá (or lamb) one and man ring (or nose ring, earring, shackle, collar, necklace) gold one

- Leningrad Codex: vayyittenu-lov ish kesitah echat ve'ish nezem zahav echad (וַיִּתְּנוּ־לֹו אִישׁ קְשִׂיטָה אֶחָת וְאִישׁ נֶזֶם זָהָב אֶחָד). Translation: and gave him man k'sitá (or lamb) one and man ring (or nose ring, earring, shackle, collar, necklace) gold one

- Targum to Job: ălôy wîhabû lêh gəbar hûrepā hădā weĕnāš qādāšā dedahăbā hād (עֲלֹוִי וִיהַבוּ לֵיהּ גְּבַר חוּרְפָא חֲדָא וֶאֱנַשׁ קַדָּשָׁא דְּדַהֲבָא חַד). Translation: elevated and gave him strong young lamb rejoice weak sacred golden meat pieces

CHAPTER 42

The Greeks translated k'sitá (קשׂיטה) as "ewe lamb" which is considered technically correct, however, the word was rarely used in Hebrew or Phoenician Canaanite and does not appear to have been used in Aramaic. The texts it survives in, are set in the Late Bronze Age, including the books of Genesis and Joshua, in both of which it was used as a monetary unit. The word is accepted as an Egyptian loanword, specifically referring to an Ancient Egyptian monetary unit that was represented as a lamb in hieroglyphs. This indicates that either the text originated in Egyptian, or the Egyptians were ruling the land when the original text was written.

The drachma was a Greek coin used from around 1100 BC, weighing approximately 4.3 grams of silver, although it is unclear if it was the correct value of the Ancient Egyptian gold lamb-shaped "coin." The presence of the word indicates that the Book of Job was likely translated into Canaanite during the New Kingdom Era, around the time that the relevant sections of Genesis and Joshua were written.

3 Codex Vaticanus: cyrios (ⲕⲨⲣⲓⲟⲥ). Translation: lord
- Aleppo Codex: Yhůh (יהוה)
- Leningrad Codex: Yhvah (יְהוָה)
- Papyrus Oxyrhynchus 3522: Yhůh (𐤉𐤄𐤅𐤄)
- Targum to Job: yeyā (יְיָ). Translation: Yhů

Papyrus Oxyrhynchus 3522 dates to the 1st century AD. It is a group of fragments of what appears to be the Septuagint's Job with the word Lord (Κύριος) replaced with Yhůh (𐤉𐤄𐤅𐤄) in Canaanite script, confirming that the original Greek translation of Job did not include the name Iaw (Ιαω).

4 Codex Vaticanus: êmeran (ΗΜΕΡΑΝ). Translation: day
- Aleppo Codex: ymymh (יְמִימָה). Translation: day
- Leningrad Codex: yemimah (יְמִימָֽה). Translation: day
- Targum to Job: yemîmā (יְמִימָא)

Her name was Jemimah in the Masoretic Text, which translates in Hebrew and Aramaic as "day." Her name in the Septuagint was Êmeran (Ημέραν), which translates as "(the) day," while in the Testament of Job it was Êmera (Ημέρα) which translates as "day." The difference between her name in the Septuagint and Testament of Job indicates they were separately translated into Greek, and her name was 'day' in both texts. As the Greeks translated the word for day, but her name was not Greek, the Aramaic and Hebrew version is imported from the Masoretic texts.

5 Codex Vaticanus: Casian (ΚΑCΙΑΝ)
- Aleppo Codex: Qsyôh (קְצִיעָה). Translation: cassia tree
- Leningrad Codex: Ketzi'ah (קְצִיעָֽה). Translation: cassia tree
- Targum to Job: qesîātā (קְצִיעֲתָא). Translation: fig
harvesting

As the name is still used in English as Cassia, the English variant is used in this translation.

6 Codex Vaticanus: Amalthias ceras (ΑΜΑΛΘΕΙΑCΚΕΡΑC). Translation: Amalthea's Horn (or Cornucopia)
- Codex Sinaiticus: Amathias ceras (ΑΜΑΘΙΑCΚΕΡΑC). Translation: Amalthea's Horn (or Cornucopia)

- Codex Alexandrinus: maltheas ceras (ΜΑΛΘΕΑⲤΚΕΡΑⲤ). Translation: Malthea's Horn (or Cornucopia)
- Codex Ephraemi Rescriptus: Amalthias ceras (ΑΜΑΛΘΙΑⲤΚΕΡΑⲤ). Translation: Amalthea's Horn (or Cornucopia)
- Septuagint manuscripts N/V: Amalthaeas ceras (ἀμαλθαίας κέρας). Translation: Amalthea's Horn (or Cornucopia)
- Septuagint manuscript 55: Amaltheas ceras (ἀμαλθέας κέρας). Translation: Amalthea's Horn (or Cornucopia)
- Septuagint manuscript 296: Amanthias ceras (ἀμανθίας κέρας). Translation: Amalthea's Horn (or Cornucopia)

- Aleppo Codex: qrn hpŭk (קרן הפוך). Translation: flipped (or inverted, backward, reversed, inside out) horn (or antler, ray, beam, corner, radiant, shining)
- Leningrad Codex: keren happuch (קֶרֶן הַפּוּךְ). Translation: flipped (or inverted, backward, reversed, inside out) horn (or antler, ray, beam, corner)
- Targum to Job: dahăwat sagî zîw yeqar appāhā hêk izmargedā (דַהֲוַת סַגִי זִיו יְקַר אַפָּהָא הֵיךְ אִזְמַרְגְדָא). Translation: from it comes great vegetation for honored bakers like emeralds (or Zambia, Zambezi)

Job's third daughter was known as Amalthea's Horn in both the Septuagint's Book of Job and the Testament of Job, meaning this was a widespread translation at the time. In Greek mythology, Amalthea was one of the foster mothers of Zeus, and her name translates as "tender goddess." The term Amalthea's Horn refers to what in Latin was called the cornucopia, a goat's horn that was endlessly overflowing with fruit and grain. The legend surrounding Amalthea's Horn, involves the infant Zeus accidentally breaking off one of her horns, which then became a cornucopia. This event was set in the ancient Minoan civilization, on Mount Ida in Crete, and therefore, where the Canaanite god Kothar-wa-Khasis originated, so it is possible that the daughter was named after the cornucopia. The translator of the Aramaic targum interpreted the name the same way, although described the cornucopia instead of using the Greek name.

Subscription

This man is described in the Aramaic book[1] as living in the land of Aysitidi, on the borders of Edom and Arabia. His name was previously Jobab, and he had an Arabian wife. He fathered a son whose name was Ennon. He was the son of his father Zare, one of the sons of Esau, and his mother was Bosorrha, and so he was the fifth from Abraham. These were the kings who reigned in Edom, which country he also ruled over:

First was Balak, the son of Beor, and the name of his city was Dinhabah.

After Balak, Jobab, who is called Job.

After him Hushim, who was governor of the country of Teman.

After him Hadad, the son of Bered, who destroyed Midian in the plain of Moab. The name of his city was Gethaim.

His friends who came to him were Eliphaz, of the children of Esau, king of the Temanites, Bildad sovereign of the Shuhites, and King Zophar of the Minaeans.

Subscription Notes

1 The following synopsis of the Aramaic (Syrian) book has some of the same information as the Testament of Job, but also

some notable differences. One difference is that the Testament of Job reports he was a son of Esau, and a brother of Nahor, who is mentioned as the author of the text, while this Syrian book apparently listed Job as the Grandson of Esau through his son Zare (Ζαρὲ). As the Testament of Job appears to be a Second Temple Era work, yet includes the much older Song of Eliphaz, is it plausible that this Syrian book was its source.

Septuagint Manuscripts

The following is a list of the Septuagint manuscripts referenced in the notes for this book.

LXX א (Codex Sinaiticus) is dated to the 4th century. Sections are currently located at British Library (Add. 43725) in London, Leipzig University (Gr. 1) in Leipzig, National Library of Russia (Gr. 2, Gr. 259, Gr. 843, and Fonds. d. Ges. f. alte Lit. Oct 156) in St, Petersburg, and Saint Catherine's Monastery (MΓ 1) on Mount Sinai.

LXX A (Codex Alexandrinus) is dated to the 5th century. It is currently located at the British Library (Royal 1 D. VIII) in London.

LXX B (Codex Vaticanus) is dated to the 4th century. It is currently located at the Vatican Library (Gr. 1209) in Vatican City.

LXX C (Codex Ephraemi Rescriptus) is dated to the 5th century. It is currently located at the Bibliothèque nationale de France (Gr. 9) in Paris.

LXX N/V (Codex Basiliano-Vaticanus + Codex Venetus) is dated to the 5th century. It is currently located at the Vatican Library (Regin. Gr. 2106) in Vatican City and the Biblioteca Marciana (Gr. 1) in Venice.

LXX 46 is dated to the 13th or 14th century. It is currently located at the Bibliothèque nationale de France (Coils. 4) in Paris.

LXX 55 is dated to the 10th century. It is currently located at the Vatican Library (Regin. Gr. 1) in Vatican City.

LXX 68 (Minuscule 205) is dated to the 15th century. It is currently located at the Biblioteca Marciana (Gr. 5) in Venice.

LXX 130 is dated to the 12th or 13th centuries. It is currently located at the Austrian National Library (Theol. Gr. 23) in Vienna.

LXX 137 is dated to the 9th century. It is currently located at the Ambrosian Library (D. 73 sup.) in Milan.

LXX 248 is dated to the 13th century. It is currently located at the Vatican Library (Vat. Gr. 346) in Vatican City.

LXX 249 is dated to the 13th century. It is currently located at the Vatican Library (Pii. II Gr. 1) in Vatican City.

LXX 250 is dated to the 13th century. It is currently located at the Bavarian State Library (Gr. 148) in Munich.

LXX 251 is dated to the 14th century. It is currently located at the Laurentian Library (Plut. V 27) in Florence.

LXX 252 is dated to the 10th century. It is currently located at the Laurentian Library (Plut. VIII 27) in Florence.

LXX 254 is dated to the 10th century. It is currently located at the Vatican Library (Gr. 337) in Vatican City.

LXX 261 is dated to 1323. It is currently located at the Laurentian Library (Plut. VII 30) in Florence.

LXX 336 is dated to the 14th century. It is currently located at the Monastery of Iviron (555) on Mount Athos.

LXX 337 is dated to the 14th century. It is currently located at the Monastery of Iviron (615) on Mount Athos.

LXX 339 is dated to the 11th century. It is currently located at the Vatopedi (8) on Mount Athos.

LXX 406 is dated to the 8th century. It is currently located at the Patriarchal Library (Σταυροῦ 36) in Jerusalem.

LXX 543 is dated to 1186. It is currently located at the National Library of France (Gr. 11) in Paris.

LXX 575 is dated to the 13th century. It is currently located at the National Library of France (Gr. 396) in Paris.

LXX 620 is dated to the 13th century. It is currently located at the Pelekete monastery (419) on Patmos Island.

LXX 637 is dated to the 11th century. It is currently located at the Biblioteca Casanatense (241) in Rome.

LXX 644 is dated to the 11th century. It is currently located at the Vatican Library (Barber. gr. 369) in Vatican City.

LXX 705 is dated to the 13th or 14th century. It is currently located at the National Library of Greece (2410) in Athens.

LXX 728 is dated to the 14th or 15th centuries. It is currently located at the Biblioteca Marciana (Append I 13) in Venice.

LXX 739 is dated to the 10th century. It is currently located at the Biblioteca Marciana (Gr. 534) in Venice.

LXX 754 is dated to the 11th century. It is currently located at the Austrian National Library (Theol. Gr. 147) in Vienna.

LXX 795 is dated to the 12th or 13th centuries. It is currently located at the Monastery of Great Lavra (Γ 51) on Mount Athos.

LXX 797 is dated to the 13th or 14th century. It is currently located at the Benaki Museum (53) in Athens.

LXX 857 is dated to the 1st century. It is currently located at the Sackler Library (Papyrus Oxyrhynchus 3522) in Oxford.

Alternative Translations

The following is a list of alternative translations that were used for comparative analysis. Both the Peshitta and Coptic translations are believed to have been heavily based on the Septuagint, although they do inherit relics of older Imperial Aramaic translations, or imports from the Hebrew translation.

The Leningrad Codex is dated to 1008 (or 1009) AD. It is currently located at the National Library of Russia (Firkovich B 19 A) in St. Petersburg. The Leningrad Codex is the oldest complete copy of the Hebrew scriptures used within Judaism.

Peshitta: The Syriac translation of the Christian bible. The Old Testament was translated from older Aramaic and Hebrew sources during the late 2nd century AD.

The Aramaic Targum to Job is generally accepted as having been compiled between 1 and 600 AD, although the surviving copies are all in Babylonian Aramaic.

Bohairic manuscripts are translations of the Septuagint into Bohairic (also known as Memphitic), one of the six dialects of Coptic, the classical era form of the Egyptian language. These dialects were written slightly differently, and therefore words transliterated into Coptic retain slightly different pronunciations, reflecting the different source texts used. Bohairic originated in the western Nile Delta of northern Egypt. The earliest Bohairic manuscripts date to the 4th century, however, the majority of texts come from the 9th century or later. Bohairic is the dialect used today as the liturgical language of the Coptic Orthodox Church, although Sahidic was used before the 11th century. Translations of the Septuagint were made into at least five of the Coptic dialects, however, complete copies only survive in Bohairic and Sahidic.

Sahidic manuscripts are translations of the Septuagint into Sahidic (also known as Thebaic), one of the six dialects of Coptic, the classical era form of the Egyptian language. Sahidic was the dominant form of Coptic used before the 11th century, and is believed to have originated in the region around Hermopolis, at the boundary between Upper and Lower Egypt. Translations of the Septuagint into Sahidic are known to have existed by the 4th century, however, early non-dialect specific translations are generally accepted as having been made as early as the 1st century AD, with some scholars suggesting the 1st century BC. The early non-dialect specific forms of Coptic are generally grouped with Sahidic, as Sahidic did not have a standardized spelling until the 6th century.

The Vetus Latina are the old Latin translations of the Septuagint and other Israelite texts that predate Jerome's Latin Orthodox Bible in the 5th century. Some of the texts appear to have been translated directly from Aramaic or Hebrew source texts, however, most appear to have been translations from the Greek translations.

Dead Sea Scrolls

The following is a list of the Dead Sea Scrolls mentioned in the notes for this book. Most are held by the Israel Museum in Jerusalem.

DSS 4Q99 (4QJob^a) is dated to the Hasmonean Dynasty (140 to 37 BC).

DSS 4Q101 (4QpaleoJob^c) is dated to the Hellenistic Era in Judea (332 to 165 BC).

Also Available

ALSO AVAILABLE

ENOCH AND METATRON SERIES:
- Books of Enoch Collection
- Books of Enoch and Metatron Collection
- Books of Metatron Collection
- Secrets of Enoch

OTHER TRANSLATIONS:
- Apocalypses of Ezra
- Arabic Maccabees
- Hebrew Maccabees
- Life of Adam and Eve
- Memories of the New Kingdom
- Septuagint's Esther and the Vetus Latina Esther
- Septuagint's Ezekiel and the Ba'al Cycle
- Septuagint's Job and the Testament of Job
- Septuagint's Proverbs and the Wisdom of Amenemope
- Syriac Maccabees – Deuterocanonical Books
- The Amarna Letters
- Testaments of the Patriarchs Collection
- Tobit and Ahikar
- Ugaritic Texts: Ba'al Cycle
- Wisdom of Ahikar

Milton Keynes UK
Ingram Content Group UK Ltd.
UKHW030947071224
452128UK00011B/514